Stop, Snap, and Switch

Train Your Brain to Unleash
Your Limitless Life

By Krista Mashore

Visit KristaMashore.com/SSSBook to get access to your Stop Snap & Switch resources

- Stop Snap & Switch Playbook
- Copies of graphics mentioned throughout the book
- Exclusive training videos
- 5 Day Limitless Life Challenge

SCAN ME

Acknowledgements

To my loving husband Steve: Thank you so much for your loyalty, your kindness, and your commitment to our marriage. Words cannot describe how much that means to me and how our love makes me a better person. Thank you for all of your support and understanding in my crazy obsession with getting my message out to make a positive difference in the world! I love you!

To my precious daughters, Jaylin and Kayli: Watching you grow into beautiful, talented, caring young women has been the biggest blessing of my life! I am so proud of both of you and I know you have bright futures ahead. I love you both to the moon and back and forth 100 million times!

To Dad and Mom: Thank you for believing in me even when I didn't believe in myself. The strong moral values you taught me have helped me stay true to myself, even when it wasn't easy. Thank you for your love and support over the years. You are rock stars to me and I love you both so much!

To all of my coaches and mentors too numerous to mention: You know who you are! Thank you so much for helping me take quantum leaps in my business and personal growth! I know you'll see your teachings in the pages of this book. Because of what you've taught me, I'm now able to make an impact on the world and I am so grateful.

To my readers: Thank you so much for taking your precious time to read this book. Please know that I am rooting for you and your success! I believe in you and I appreciate you more than you'll ever know.

Foreword

Over the last 20 years of my life, I've had a chance to work with high-level entrepreneurs who have a passion and a mission to change the world. When they come into my world, one of the very first things I always tell them is "You're just one funnel away from success." Obviously, success is different for every single person. But specifically with my audience, I'm focusing on "How can they get their message out to the market and change the lives of the people that they've been called to serve?"

Reading Krista's new book, *Stop, Snap and Switch*, I'm excited because her message is similar. Not so much that "you're one funnel away from success." But that you are one *mindset shift* away from having the business, the career, and the life that you really want.

Most people think that success in business is all about the tactics and the strategy. While those things are important, psychology is actually more important. I remember one of my very first live events where Tony Robbins was our keynote speaker. He got on stage and told us all that success in *anything* in life is 20% tactics and 80% psychology. And it's the psychology, the mindset, where most people get tripped up.

I first met Krista when she had just joined my Inner Circle Coaching Program. She had already had a lot of success in her real estate business. In fact, I think there are few people on this planet who had more success than she did. But she was there because she wanted to make a change and shift in her career. She wanted to go from being a successful agent to teaching other people how to have success like she did. Very few people cross this chasm, from focusing on their own personal and business success to focusing on making a contribution to other people. I could tell she was nervous and excited. I could also tell that she was very similar to me, that she felt a strong calling and desire to change people's lives. The difference was that she didn't really know how. So, she came into our world and she invested a whole bunch of money to learn how to do it.

I still remember the very first meeting when she got up. She had such a sense of urgency. She didn't want to just help other people. She wanted to help other people *now*! In fact, after our first meeting, I kept getting messages from her that she was frustrated. It was going too slow, it wasn't working. But within just a few months, it clicked. I watched her new business go from a startup to winning her very first Two Comma Club Award (meaning she made $1 million) in just a matter of months.

You may think that Krista is an overnight success, and from the outside, it looks like that. But Krista understands something most people don't. She got the exact same strategies and tactics that I've given to hundreds of thousands of entrepreneurs. So, what made her move faster? What made her have success so quickly when it takes others a lot longer, and many honestly *never* have any success at all? The reason is the things and principles she teaches inside this book: the mindset shifts you need to have so you can actually achieve success.

The mindset shifts you'll learn in this book will help you in all areas of your life, not just business. It'll help you in your relationships, it'll help you with your family, it'll help you with your health. It'll help you with any goals that you want to achieve.

One other cool thing is the fact that Krista is literally a product of her product. You can see the results that she's gotten for herself and for her students, year in and year out. In fact, in the last few years, she's won eight of our Two Comma Club Awards (meaning she created 8 different sales funnels that each generated over $1 million in sales) and she also won our Two Comma Club C Award, (meaning she generated over $25 million in sales online). How does she do it?

She soaks up knowledge like a sponge and then she implements like crazy. She has a positive attitude, and she keeps her priorities straight. She doesn't always do everything perfectly the very first time. I've seen her make mistakes and fall down and mess up. But the thing that's unique about Krista is that when those setbacks happen, she looks at the situation then she tries to figure out the shifts and the changes she needs to make to be successful. She gets back up and she attacks it again. And she does it relentlessly over and over and over again until success is inevitable.

I always tell people that when you're starting a new business, you need to find your dream customers and try to serve them. Krista literally is one of my dream customers. She's someone who works hard, focuses on other people, and implements quickly.

I've had a chance to work with a lot of high achievers in tons of different markets. There are very few people who are driven as Krista, which is shown by what she's been able to achieve, both professionally and personally. In *Stop, Snap and Switch*, she pulls out all the stops and shares with you all the mindset tools that she has used herself to help build a phenomenal business and an amazing personal life.

I know how much effort goes into writing a book and I know what she put into this book for you. My hope is that you read these pages that she so painstakingly wrote for you and that you look at this book as a personal consultation from Krista to you. I hope that you listen to, and actually implement the things she teaches you. Value it as if you just paid her a $100,000 for her insights and experience, and if you do that, you'll get 10 times more than that out of this book and you'll be able to achieve incredible success in all areas of your life.

Russell Brunson

Co-Founder of ClickFunnels

Foreword

I'm always saying that "the biggest enemy is the inner me." That's why I love what Krista teaches in this book. It's everything I believe in and teach to my eXp family. We're both the problem and the solution. And if you think about it, that's great! Because if the only thing holding you back is *you*, you can do something about it, right?

In *Stop, Snap and Switch*, Krista shows you exactly *what* you can do about it. She teaches you how to turn a life of quiet desperation into one that is incredible. And she keeps it simple, explaining things in a way that is easy to understand and entertaining to read.

What makes Krista effective at coaching people and writing books like this is that she's 100% authentic. She will tell you about all the ways that she's not perfect and how her background was no fairy tale. She'll tell you straight out that becoming more than who you've always been is no walk in the park. It requires hard work. But it's hard work that she's done herself and that she can guide you through.

After just a couple of months of knowing Krista, I was inviting her up on stage to speak at my events. Partly, it was because she was doing such incredible things in building her business. But it was also because I can see that she is truly passionate about helping others. She has a generous heart and serves others unconditionally. Krista has been a blessing in my life, and I know this book will be a blessing in yours.

So, get off of the couch and onto your feet!! Into the Battle and into the Heat!! Start reading this book and make your life sweet!!

—Brent Gove

eXp Realty, 30,000+ agents in his organization

CONTENTS

Introduction

*"Most people live and die with their music still unplayed.
They never dare to try."*
- Mary Kay Ash

Not too long ago, I heard a story explaining how they train elephants. In India, where elephants are used for transportation and labor, the elephants have to be trained and domesticated. And their trainers don't want them wandering around and destroying crops or buildings. So, the first thing the trainers do is to train the elephants to stay in a certain area when they are not working. When elephants are just babies, they tie them to a stake using a heavy rope. Now when the baby elephant starts out, it weighs about 200 pounds so you would think they'd be strong enough to break a rope. But they're still awkward and just learning to use their trunks and bodies as babies. So, though they try as hard as they can, they can't break free from the rope. And after a while they stop even trying. By the time the elephants are fully grown, the trainers know they can just use a skinny, weak rope to keep them from wandering. Why? Because even though these huge elephants could *easily* break that rope, they're so convinced that they *can't* that they don't even try! Crazy, huh?

But do you ever feel like that? Like somewhere inside you, you *know* you have the strength, talent, and skill to do something, but you can't get yourself to even try?

The elephant training reminded me of another story I heard about a white tiger named Mohini. Mohini lived in a zoo in one of those 12 foot by 12 foot cages. The tiger spent years and years in that cage, pacing back and forth like you used to see lions and tigers and cheetahs do in a zoo. Finally, the zoo modernized and built a great, big open habitat for Mohini that had trees and hills and places to run. You know what happened when they put her in it? She ran to a corner by the fence and started pacing in a 12 foot by 12 foot area—and she hardly ever left that area until the day she died.

Have you ever felt like Mohini? Somewhere inside, you *know* there's a bigger world out there for you, but no matter what you try, you can't seem to get out of the smaller world you're living in?

The elephant and Mohini were confined by what was in their heads. Neither of them really had to keep living such small, unfulfilling lives. But their minds, the beliefs and habits that had been conditioned in, had enough power to make a 4 ton elephant stay tied to a tiny string and an adult tiger to keep pacing her invisible cage even after she was free. It's so sad! Yet I see way too many people who are doing the exact same thing—living lives that are small, and stressful, and unsatisfying *because their minds convince them they have* to.

And I almost ended up down the same road.

Starting Life in My Personal Cage

When I look at my own life, I can tell you if I hadn't learned to cut the rope and leap out of the cage by mastering my mindset—how I look at the world and especially how I think about myself—I would definitely not have the success and happiness I have today. It's scary for me to even think about what I would have become if I still believed what I believed about myself when I was growing up! Today, people see me on stage and think, "Oh, Krista's successful and confident because

> *"Don't let your circumstance dictate your finance, create your finance."*
> **- Krista Mashore**

she's got that pretty long blond hair (which is fake, by the way). Look at her classy, expensive shoes ($79 from DSW). She's just a naturally great speaker (I used to be so scared talking in front of people that I'd literally forget my own name!). And she's always so positive (yeah, thanks to years of counseling and personal work)."

Whatever I might look like to you, I need to share with you where I really started. Why? I've shared personal stories before, like about my marriage falling apart and how that lit a fire under my rear to build an incredible real estate career. But in 2020, I was listening to my mentor, Russell Brunson, and he was talking about how important your story is and how, when you share about your past, it can help people. We all have limiting beliefs of what we can or can't do, and when you share your own issues, it gives people hope that they can overcome their own. I remember sitting there thinking, "Oh my gosh, I haven't been telling the story I really *should* be telling. The story about my childhood." See, I'm the girl who wet her bed till she was 10. I'm the girl who had severe learning disabilities and I wasn't able to read until the 4th grade. In 2nd grade, I was put in a special education class for two years. I'm the girl who ended up in juvenile hall, then a group home, and then in foster care. I'm the girl who hasn't lived at home since I was 13.

And I'm the girl who was abused by a parent.

Before I share my story, I want you to know that I am very, very close to both my mom and dad. My dad is one of my best friends. My mom is the most loyal, loving person ever. But my mom had her own childhood challenges that affected the way she raised me. I remember getting on the plane after hearing Russell and realizing I needed to share this story. I wrote my mom a letter on a yellow piece of paper, and I was crying while writing that letter, asking my mom if it was okay that I shared what had happened to me as a child. I wanted her permission to share my story because she was a part of it. I didn't want her to be hurt and she's done a lot to help me with my healing. I love her.

My biggest passion is to help people and after hearing Russell's teachings at Funnel Hacking Live, I knew I had to share my story. To make a true impact on the world, I had to show them where I came from, that I was just like them. Someone who came from humble beginnings, who didn't always have the money or whatever people feel is important. So, I wrote my mom the letter to ask her if I could share our story. This was so dear and raw to my heart that it took me 2 weeks just to give it to her! She didn't respond for two weeks (usually we talk or text several times a week). And then one day she called me and said, "Let's have lunch and talk about the letter." We met for lunch, but the letter was never mentioned. Still, I knew that was my green light to share my story. My mom continues to put my needs above her own. She has done everything she can to help heal my wounds and help me continue to grow.

See, as a child, it was almost like I lived in two families. We had a very happy loving family. Yet underneath, I experienced physical abuse that only my mom and I knew about. By the time I turned 13, I couldn't handle it anymore. I started running away from home. I lived in abandoned buildings. I lived in my friend's parents' RVs. I lived in their closets at night while their parents were sleeping, and the parents had no idea that I was there.

Eventually, my parents or the police would always find me. I'd run away again. They'd find me. I'd run away again. I just couldn't handle the abuse anymore. This went on for over a year. I cannot describe to you all of the scary experiences I found myself in during that year. To this day, I know that I truly had a guardian angel by my side, keeping me safe from the real bad guys out there. I truly believe those angels protected me so that one day I could help others who have had issues (which is *all* of us!) and so I could be a catalyst of hope and inspiration to help others find the happiness and fulfillment we all deserve.

Finally, one day I broke the law. My best friend and I ended up breaking into my eighth grade PE locker room and stealing all the girls' clothes and stealing their lunch money because we had no food and no clothes. We got caught. My best friend and I were sent to juvenile hall. When we got there, I remember thinking, "I don't belong here". I remember seeing this girl with bright red hair who was like six feet tall! I watched her grab another girl's head in the bathroom and slam her head into the porcelain toilet. Blood was just gushing everywhere. And I remember thinking to myself, "I'm going to die in here. I don't belong in this place. I'm going to die here."

I spent three and a half months in juvenile hall. When I finally got out, I was sent to a group home for troubled girls in Cottonwood, California. Every day we would get dropped off for school in this big, green bus that had "Hidden Hills Group Home for Girls" plastered all over it. That bus announced to the rest of the school, "Hey, we're screw ups. Don't talk to us. Ignore us, chastise us, make fun of us." It was a horrible year. High school is a pretty crucial time when just about everybody feels insecure and vulnerable, right? Well, every day when I got dropped off in that bus, I felt like a total loser! It was just another blow to my confidence, one more thing that made me feel unworthy and "less than." It's a feeling I carried with me for many years until I learned to deal with it. The thing is that it never completely disappears. You have to continually face and battle those feelings.

I stayed in the group home for a year. I ended up becoming a peer counselor, one of the youngest teen counselors that they had ever had. Then I got sent back home. Though the physical abuse had stopped, things had not changed. There was so much history, so much that was unspoken, so much the family didn't know about, I realized I had to go.

So, I called my probation officer, and I told him I needed to leave. My dad didn't understand what was happening. I remember him standing on the driveway, begging me not to leave. "Krista, we love you. Whatever it is, we can work it out. Please stay, please don't go." I was sobbing. My dad was crying. I couldn't tell him why I had to leave, and he didn't know about the history between my mom and me. He worked so hard to support us and to be a good father. (Later, I found out the only time he had ever cried was when his mom died and when I left home that day.) I was so sad having to leave my brothers and my parents. And I loved my mom, but I just couldn't stay there. While my foster dad drove me to my new home in his silver Toyota truck, I cried the whole way. I cried myself to sleep for months. Even today when I speak of it, tears come to my eyes, just as they are right now as I am writing this. I spent the next three years in a foster home. When I turned 18 and graduated from high school, my foster parents kicked me out of the house because the money quit coming in.

You see, when you go through physical abuse from a parent, it is psychologically very damaging. As a kid and even as an adult, a lot of crazy stuff can go on in your head about it and what the abuse says about you as a person. It's taken a lot of work on my part to believe in myself, to break out of that cage and to believe that I'm worthy and deserving of love and deserving of good things.

When I got out of the foster home, I went through a lot of counseling. I remember sitting in my family's driveway because I wanted to ask my mom to tell the family why I had left. My leaving had caused a total, horrible ripple effect. My mother went through a lot of pain because the memories that she had suppressed from her own childhood came up during the years of my absence. The family was a wreck once I left. I felt as though my brothers blamed me for it, which made me feel even worse about myself. I wanted the family to know the *real* reason I left was not because I wanted to be wild, crazy and free.

I sat in that driveway for a few hours crying and fearful about confronting her. Finally, I got the courage to confront her. "Mom, I need you to tell Dad what happened. He thinks I left because I just wanted to party. I need you to tell him why I really left." Mom was nothing but amazing. It was hard for her, but she went to counseling with me. She admitted what she had done, and it helped me heal. And she told the whole family so the family was able to heal.

Just a couple of years ago, Mom broke down crying. It was one of those heart-wrenching scenes in a movie. She was balled up like a baby, crying so hard that she couldn't stop for hours. She was so upset and distraught that we had to call a close friend who was like a 2nd son to her to calm her down. The pain of what she had done was overwhelming her. "I'm so sorry for what I did to you. I feel so guilty."

I told her, "Mom, I would not change my childhood for anything." And I mean it. I don't want her to feel guilty about it at all. Everything that happened to me made me who I am and made it possible for me to help as many people as I can today because it makes me more relatable. I'm grateful in a way for all the things my life has brought me. No regrets and no guilt. (By the way, guilt is one of the most useless emotions that we carry. It just holds us back and keeps us caged.) Forgive yourself, be better, and move on!!

I started as a baby elephant tied to a stake by a rope. No one set me up to succeed. Nobody gave me money. Nobody bought me my first car. I had to get a loan to put myself through college. I paid for my own car, my insurance, my rent, my food, everything. I've had to work really hard my whole life.

And most importantly, I had to work my tail off to change what I believed about myself and what was possible for me. I could have stayed tied to that stake and settled for my limiting story that "You're the girl who wet the bed until she was 10. You were in a group home. You were in a foster home. You were abused. Nobody loves you. You're not good enough. You're not worthy. Your former husband cheated on you." (I'll get into that story later on.) But those limiting beliefs would not let me be where I am now. Our biggest enemy can be ourselves and what we believe about ourselves.

Everybody has had some kind of issue, whether it's physical or verbal abuse, difficulty in school, physical problems, feeling like an outsider, divorce, trauma, failure in business, growing up in poverty, PTSD from being in a war zone—the list goes on and on! Even with an upbringing that's very loving, you can be taught messages like, "Stay safe and don't take risks" or "Nice people finish last" or "Try to fit in with people" or "Don't stand out because someone can shoot you down." They mean well. They're trying to protect you from some kind of pain they imagine you might have. But really, they're instilling fear and limiting beliefs that will just hold you back.

I didn't start out as the person you may see on stage, or hear on a podcast, or the person who writes books or the person who can run two multi-million dollar companies. I've had to work to become this person and to believe in myself. And I believe that sharing my story is going to help make an impact on others. It will help people see that anybody can do anything that they put their mind to, even with a background like mine. We all have stories and excuses. And we all have the *choice* to change our story, change our beliefs, and change our mindset. You might be familiar with the saying, "Let your mess become your message." Well, let's make our messes, the ones all of us have, and make them our message. Let's choose to let our past, no matter what it is, not *define* us in a negative way, but be the *catalyst* for the best life we can imagine, the life that we deserve

I don't care how skilled you are at your business, how great your tactics and strategies are, or how awesome your product or service is. And it doesn't matter how talented, beautiful, smart, or attractive you are or aren't. It doesn't matter if you were born into lots of money or you started out flat broke. It's your thoughts and your mindset that will make or break you in all areas of your life. Why?

Because *what and how you think* affects your *emotions* and leads to your *actions* and your actions create your *results* in life.

Your thinking includes your attitudes, your beliefs, and your philosophy about life. It affects your mood, emotions and energy level. Your action is made up of your habits, routines and rituals, and how you implement your ideas and intentions. Your life is made up of the results you get, your successes, your growth and satisfaction with life. (To help you remember, here's a cool graphic called Thoughts to Action you can download at KristaMashore.com/SSSBook.)

Thinking >> Actions >> Results >> Your Life

MINDSET MATTERS

YOUR WAYS OF
THINKING

ATTITUDES
BELIEFS
PHILOSOPHIES

↓

SHAPES YOUR
ACTION

HABITS
ROUTINES + RITUALS
IMPLEMENTATION

↓

CREATES YOUR
LIFE

RESULTS
SUCCESS
GROWTH

What has made the most difference in my career, my finances, my personal life, and even my phys- ical health has been strengthen- ing my mindset and working with the most powerful organ of my body, my brain.

> What has made the most difference in my career, my finances, my personal life, and even my physical health has been strengthening my mindset and working with the most powerful organ of my body, my brain.

As I'm writing this, my com- pany recently got our 2CCC Award for generating $25 mil- lion in sales online from ClickFunnels and eight 2CC awards (each for generating $1 million in online sales). We've made $37 million online in just over four years. So, it's not surprising that people come to me and say, "Teach me how to run a Facebook ad and how to build a mil- lion-dollar funnel." The truth is that I can teach you step by step how to do that, but if you don't work on your mindset and your belief in yourself, and all aspects of being the best version of yourself, you'll never be able to do a million-dollar funnel or make a million dollars.

You see, initially when I first started coaching, I gave people all the skills and tools they wanted. I taught them how to build funnels, create Facebook campaigns, and design marketing plans. I thought I was giv- ing them all these things that they needed to succeed but I didn't focus at all on mindset. And they were getting some results but not nearly what I thought they should.

I started doing a different training called a five-day challenge, and 85% of what I taught in that five day challenge was about mindset. It was working on their limiting beliefs, having them identify those be- liefs that were holding them back. I had them write down these beliefs then we burned them. Next, we had them turn those limiting beliefs around and change what they were saying to themselves. So, "I'm too old to change careers" turned into, "My age and wisdom is going to help me excel at this." Or "I'm too young to excel at my job so early on." Turned into, "My youth is going to give me a more competitive edge because of my skill with technology." Next, we taught them how to insert these more positive beliefs and had them do daily practices and activities that would strengthen their mindset. And guess what? Within a five-day timeframe, these people were experiencing more suc- cess than my other students were! Even though they knew *less* about the tactical tools and strategies than my other students, these 5-day challenge folks who had worked on mindset outperformed them!

It became really obvious that I had to start with the mindset and incorporate the mindset into it every single week of my coaching in conjunction with giving them all the tactics and the strategies. That's when we started seeing our students have massive, massive success.

Why did mindset make such a difference? I love Tony Robbins' teachings and I saw him do a presentation recently where he explained it using this chart that he calls the Success Cycle:

THE SUCCESS CYCLE

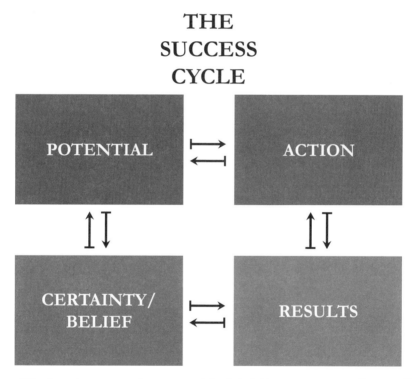

All of us have amazing potential, right? But not many of us really *believe* in our potential. In fact, many of us believe really strongly in the opposite, our limitations. We put so much faith in our limitations that when it comes to taking action, we tap into only a tiny bit of our potential. We hesitate, do a crappy job or don't even start at all. As you can imagine (and may have seen in your own life), that wimpy action leads to pretty rotten results. Then, because we got rotten results, our belief in our limitations becomes even stronger. So, we tap into even *less* of our potential, take even wimpier action, and get even crummier results. Then we believe even *less* in ourselves. Then when we try it again, we give it even less effort (because we don't believe) and we get even worse results. Then we tell ourselves again, "See this doesn't work." But really it didn't work because we didn't believe it would in the first place so we didn't really give it any effort. It's a vicious cycle, and the perfect roadmap to make sure you *never* get what you want!

And it all started with your beliefs, your mindset.

What we need to do is to strengthen your belief in yourself so that you're *certain* that you have great potential and that you can achieve whatever it is you want. When you feel that kind of certainty, you take fearless, ferocious action. When you take ferocious action that is *effective* action, you get some positive results. We'll talk about effective action later in the book.) Then, when you get positive results, your belief and certainty grow stronger. Much better cycle to be on, right?

The key that really successful people know is that you can't wait until something *proves* to you that you can succeed. You can't wait for circumstances to start believing in yourself and having certainty that you *can* achieve what you want. You have to believe it *before* you see it, or you will never see it.

That may sound impossible but that's what this book is all about. Training that positive belief and certainty into you *before* circumstances prove you right. Right now, your brain is responding to your beliefs and maybe your certainty in your limitations. (I'll explain more about how the brain works in the next section.) So, throughout this book, I'll give you some ways to shake up and remove those negative beliefs. Then I'll show you a powerful way to build up your positive belief and an unwavering certainty that you *can and will* achieve what you desire. From that strong belief, you'll feel eager and urgent about taking any action you need to take. You'll find a way no matter what to get to where you want to be. This is the secret to momentum and with a tsunami of momentum, you can't help but be carried to success.

Let's just look at one tiny aspect of mindset, a specific belief and how it can impact you. Say, you believe that it's absolutely critical to avoid any kind of failure or mistake. With that belief, you'd probably spend most of your time analyzing, calculating, what-if'ing, and not tapping your amazing creative potential. You'd probably avoid making decisions as long as possible. You'd be slow to act—or avoid acting altogether! I could teach you all the strategies in the world, but if your ship actually came in, you'd miss the boat while you worried about what to pack!

But what if you had the belief that everyone meets a few failures and makes a few mistakes along the path to creating the life they want? What if you had an *unshakeable confidence* that you *will* achieve your goal even though you might have some hiccups along the way? You'd make decisions quickly and spend much more time implementing than worrying. You wouldn't wait for the perfect plan. You'd take action when you were "ready enough" and learn from your mistakes. And when your ship came in, you'd swim out to meet it!

Which mindset is more likely to lead to success and a fulfilling life? Which is more likely to help you find your soul mate or launch a successful business? Which is more likely to keep you on track in your fitness program or help you make the money you want to make? Which is more likely to help you grow as a person?

You're supposed to "ready, aim, fire." But many people fool around getting ready while others are going for the perfect aim but they *never* fire. The more times you fire, the more opportunities you have to be successful. You may miss the mark along the way, but because you tried more than the average person, you have more successes. It all starts with your belief.

When your body isn't healthy, it doesn't function well and it can't support you in doing what you need to do physically, right? Well, it's the same with your mindset. If your mindset isn't healthy, it can't function to help you do what you need to do mentally and emotionally. A strong mindset is important at any time. But NOW is your time to do something to strengthen it. How do I know? Because something nudged you to pick up this book. Something is telling you it's time to get on with your life and move toward the life you deserve.

This belief that you need to ready/aim, ready/aim, ready/aim, and have it all perfect before you fire is just one tiny belief. Think of all the zillions of beliefs you have. Which of your beliefs are acting like a skinny rope or an invisible cage and keeping you from becoming who you could be?

One of my all-time favorite books is *Think and Grow Rich* by Napoleon Hill. I think it should be mandatory reading for every kid in high school. It has so much about mindset in it as well as success principles that can be applied to just about anything from business to athletics to relationships. If you haven't read it, you really should. If it's been a while, read it again. In fact, reading that book is one of the reasons I'm writing this one, and also why I ventured out so quickly to leave my real estate career and start coaching. Napoleon Hill interviewed the most successful people of his time and wrote about traits and success principles these multi-millionaires had in common. It wasn't that they were particularly smart or well-educated. It wasn't the type of business they had. What they had in common was the type of *mindset* that caused them to act in certain ways which resulted in their amazing successes. And one of the coolest things about all of the principles that successful people use is that they are not *born* with these qualities and principles. They learned them—and so can you.

And it's not just about business success. Your mindset also makes a huge difference in your relationships and your quality of life. Think about a person who is constantly down and negative and believes they are unattractive and unlovable. How likely are they to find a partner and solid friendships? Now think about someone who is upbeat and confident, who believes they deserve good relationships. Aren't they much more likely to attract the partner they desire and the friendships that support and nourish them? What about quality of life? If you be-lieve you have to work your fingers to the bone and be stressed all the time to be successful, what kind of life does that create?

Being the best person you can be, being the best mate you can be, being the best parent you can be, all of that has to do with mindset. I believe more than anything, *mindset is more important than skillset*. To be truly fulfilled in life, I believe that you need to be connected to your core values and live your life by them. I believe you need to be con-stantly evolving and growing and being the best version of yourself that you can. We're all human and none of us are saints. We don't need to be. We just need to keep trying to do what's right and what feels true to our values. And we need to believe in ourselves.

How to Get the Most Out of This Book

In this book, I'll be offering a ton of tips and techniques that I've learned over the years from some of the truly great teachers, coaches, and trainers. I know that every single one is effective for building and maintaining a healthy mindset based on my own experience and the experience of my students. And while I'm really happy to share this knowledge with you, I have to tell you that knowledge without action does nothing! People say that knowledge is power, but I'd say that knowledge alone is the booby prize. It's the *implementation on the knowledge* you learn that is power. We've got to take ACTION!!

I look around and notice that most people aren't really willing to do what it takes to succeed. They just aren't. If you think about it, most people don't live the life of their dreams. Most people in life are not fit and healthy. Most people are not making the kind of income that they want to make. Most people are not as happy and don't have as much energy and enthusiasm as they'd like. They're in ho-hum relationships with their partner, their kids, and their friends.

If you want to become the exception, not the rule, it all comes down to mindset. And to re-train your mindset, you have to actually *do* the techniques I'm sharing with you. They're not hard. They're simple. They are small steps you can take, tiny habits you can develop that will make an incredible difference in your life. Small positive actions done consistently are powerful no matter what you're trying to achieve! It might feel like adding them to your daily routine is just piling more on your plate. But the truth is, when you do these techniques, you'll feel more energized and more able to do all you need to do.

Mahatma Gandhi was being interviewed many years ago and he said, "I have so much to accomplish today that I must meditate for two hours instead of one." He knew how important a strong mindset was, *especially* on tough super-busy days.

To help you implement what you'll learn, I've created a Limitless Abundance Playbook for you to accompany this book. (You'll find your downloadable Limitless Abundance Playbook at KristaMashore. com/SSSBook) Anytime you get an inspiring idea from reading or listening to this book, write it down. If you learn a technique or something that hits home for you, write it down in the section that says "Action Items" in your playbook.

To help you develop these small powerful habits, how about enlisting a friend or family member to join you in going through this book? Being in a Master Mind group with people who support your growth is one of Napoleon Hill's 13 success principles and the buddy system is a great tool to keep you on track. You can even start a book club and have weekly meet-ups to uplift and encourage each other. Whether it's keeping to an exercise routine or going after a goal, a buddy or support group is great for staying on track and accountable.

Jim Rohn said, "You must take personal responsibility. You cannot change the circumstances, the seasons, or the wind, but you can change yourself. That is something you have charge of." He also said, "It's not the wind that determines your destination, it's the setting of the sail."

And as I tell my students each and every day. "You are the ONLY one responsible for creating the life that you deserve."

You're in charge!

Stop, Snap, and Switch

Once you replace negative thoughts with positive ones,
you'll start having positive results.
—Willie Nelson

The Stop, Snap and Switch is a really great tool that can be used any time anywhere. The only thing you need is a rubber band or a hair tie, anything that is easy to take on and off and remove from one wrist to another. I actually had a bunch of elastic wrist bracelets made for myself and my students, but a rubber band works just as well. (If you want one of my special Stop, Snap and Switch bracelets, you can purchase one here: https://www.amazon.com/shop/kristamashorecoaching)

Any time you have *any* type of negative thought in your brain, you stop. That thought can be anything like, "I'm too heavy. I'm too young. I'm too old. I'm too inexperienced. I'm tired. I don't have enough energy. I don't have enough resources. My husband's an a-hole. My kids are driving me crazy. This is super-hard. I'm bad with technology." It can be any thought about any aspect of your life that isn't positive and constructive. As soon as you catch yourself, that's when you *stop* and acknowledge that you're having a negative thought and that it's not the kind of thought that will get you the life you want.

Next you *snap* your rubber band or bracelet as soon as you recognize that negative thought mentally. Don't snap the rubber band too hard. You want to feel it, but you don't need to get all black and blue! Next, you *switch* the rubber band to your other wrist, and you rephrase that negative comment into a positive one. If I'm thinking, "Man, I'm too old to go into coaching. No one is going to listen to me." I'd turn that into, "Hey, my age and experience are going to help me really truly be able to help people." So, you stop, snap, and switch the negative comment into a positive one.

As you keep doing this, you're training your brain to recognize when you're negative and also getting your brain into the habit of restating the negative into positive and shifting your mindset.

The cool thing is that once you've used this and start getting good at recognizing the negative, you can also start acknowledging yourself for anything good, like when you do something well, or you have a positive thought, or you achieve something. "I just accomplished and finished my marketing plan. Good job!" "I just complimented my husband. Awesome!" "I was really focused right now during our conversation. How great is that!" Say it out loud and switch the rubber band to the other wrist and say, "Good job!"

Recognizing all the things that you're doing well is as important as recognizing the negative. Research shows that the more that you recognize and focus on what you're doing well, the more you will do them. Your brain will start trying to find ways to support you in doing the positive things. I have a couple of mantras about this: "Success breeds success" and "What gets celebrated gets replicated." As you're practicing to stop the negative, you also want to focus on the positive and how you can do more of the positive. The Stop, Snap and Switch works both ways. (To see a video of how it works, go to a vid-

> *Recognizing all the things that you're doing well is as important as recognizing the negative.*

eo called Stop, Snap & Switch Training at KristaMashore.com/ SSSBook)

When you do this, make sure your positive statements ring true to you. For example, if you say, "I hate cleaning the house" you probably won't believe a positive statement like, "I'm the Martha Stewart of my neighborhood," right? Instead, try something like "When I'm done the house is going to look great and I'm going to feel great about it" or "I'm a good person and my house doesn't have to be perfect."

Make it a game. Notice just how often you say or think something negative. If you live with others, ask if they'd like to join you with their own rubber bands. You'll be amazed at the ripple effect, and when other people around you are positive as well, it makes life more enjoyable for everyone. Teach your kids how to do this. Start them early. Can you imagine how your life might have been different if you had trained your brain away from negative thinking as a child?

Do the rubber band for at least a few days and you'll notice that your self-talk will naturally become more positive and that you'll instantly correct yourself whenever it's negative. After practicing, you'll notice that not only are you less negative, but you'll find yourself simply happier. Also, if you weren't able to enroll your spouse or kids into doing this with you, once they see the new excited, happy, invigorated you, they will automatically want to check it out.

What is Mindset?

So, let's get into the nitty gritty of mindset. It's not just about having happy thoughts. To really change your mindset so that it helps you get where you want to go, you need to change it at a deeper level. You need to change some fundamental limiting beliefs you have about yourself as well as some general beliefs about life that hold you back. The key is to make these changes so that they're *wired into your neurology*. You can make that happen by consistently using the Stop, Snap and Switch as well as through some other practices I'll share with you. But first, let's look at how it all works.

How Your Brain Works

I'm not even close to being a neuroscientist or a brain specialist! But because I know how critical mindset is, I've done a lot of reading on how the brain works. You don't need to be a certified mechanic to drive your car and you don't have to have years of training to "drive" your brain. Yet, there are a few things it's helpful to know. (And if you are a neuroscientist reading this, forgive my non-technical explanations!)

First of all, you have different parts of your brain. You've got two sides of the brain, the left and the right. The left side generally handles things like speech and comprehension, writing and arithmetic. The right side deals with creativity, music and artistic skills.

Then you have conscious parts of your mind that you control. You consciously decide to do something or not, like pick up a glass of water or go to a party or write a song. The unconscious part of your brain does things without any direction from you. It causes your heart to beat like crazy when you see someone you're crazy in love with. It directs all the systems needed to digest that taco you had for lunch. It stores all of your memories (the good, the bad, and the ugly!).

The unconscious part of the brain also *filters* all the input from the outside world that bombards you every day. It lit-

> *It literally decides what you need to be aware of or conscious of.*

erally decides what you need to be aware of or conscious of. Scientists say that our five senses take in about 11 billion bits *per second* from our surroundings. I don't claim to know exactly what that means but I know it's a lot! They also say that our conscious brains can only process *120 bits* of information per second. If you just do the math, that means the unconscious part of our brains has to filter out way over 10 billion bits, so our conscious minds don't blow up!

> *It decides what to cut and what to keep based on what we seem to want and what we believe.*

The brain has something called the reticular activating system (RAS). Its job is to filter out stuff you *don't* need to be aware of and bring your focus to things you *do* need to be aware of. But wait a minute, how does the RAS figure out what you do need to be consciously aware of and what you don't? It decides what to cut and what to keep based on *what we seem to want and what we believe.* For example, if you believe that everybody loves you, your RAS will filter out anyone who is giving you a snarky look or who looks annoyed with you. You literally will *not* even notice them! On the flip side, if you think everyone hates you, you'll *never* notice anyone who is smiling or trying to be friendly. Your RAS is trying to do a good job by showing you only what you believe to be true. Unfortunately, it may

> *Unfortunately, it may be filtering out the very things we need to be successful and be happy because we told it that we believe success and happiness is unlikely if not impossible for us!*

be filtering out the very things we need to be successful and be happy *because we told it that we believe success and happiness is unlikely if not impossible for us!*

When it comes to mindset, two parts of the brain that are really important to understand are the amygdala and the prefrontal cortex. The prefrontal cortex is in charge of reasoning, problem-solving, comprehension, impulse-control, creativity and perseverance—all critical to success in anything from business to relationships, right? It's the part of your brain that tells you to venture out, and that anything is possible. It encourages you to "shoot for the stars" and to take risks. It wants you to go outside of your comfort zone because it knows that's where all the good stuff happens. It's a *conscious* part of the brain which means that we're aware of what it's doing, and we can control it and direct it.

The amygdala is an ancient, unconscious part of our brain that has a heck of a lot of functions. Most importantly it stays very alert to any threats to our survival. When it senses a threat, it sets off all kinds of alarms to the rest of our nervous system. In fact, the amygdala is so good at this, that it can detect a threat even *before* we become consciously aware of it. It will go ahead and trigger all kinds of reactions in our bodies (like fight, flight or freeze) before we have a chance to say, "What's up?".

Think about when a car swerves into your lane. You veer out of the way or hit the brakes without giving your body instructions. That's because the amygdala is doing its job and keeping you alive. It's the part of our brain that kept our caveman ancestors from being eaten by hungry saber-toothed tigers— which is a good thing because without it, none of us would be here!

The problem comes in when the amygdala sees something as a threat to our survival that *isn't a threat at all*. It still sends off its alarms and we feel panicked, afraid or angry even though *consciously* we may realize that what we're facing will *not* kill us. Think of public speaking: Millions of people are terrified of it (just like I used to be and still am at times). They shake and sweat and their hearts race like crazy. But have you ever heard of anyone actually *dying* from public speaking? As a speaker, I've bombed a couple of times and while it wasn't much fun, I didn't die from it.

But the amygdala isn't very good about making the distinction between a *real* threat and something that's just outside our comfort zone. If you let your amygdala take charge, you'll never make a move. You might stay comfy in your cozy little comfort zone, but it will keep you stuck. You'll never achieve what you want to achieve or have the life you've always wanted.

> But the amygdala isn't very good about making the distinction between a real threat and something that's just outside our comfort zone.

There's a story that's told in different ways in many cultures about two wolves. Here's how I heard it: A young boy was talking to his grandmother, and she said, "We all have two wolves battling within us. One wolf is brave and kind and seeks to do good and thrive. The other wolf is fearful and hateful and seeks to hurt and destroy." The young boy thought for a moment then said, "But which wolf will win, the Good Wolf or the Bad Wolf?" The grandmother replied, "The one we feed."

Turns out, it's *not* just a fable! Neuroscientists have shown that our brains have "neuroplasticity." Our brains can actually change physically and create new neuropathways *based on what we feed them*. The neuropathways we *don't* use become very weak and die off. It's called "synaptic pruning". There's been all kinds of cool research on this, but what you really need to know is: If you feed the Bad Wolf (the amygdala) and give it a lot of your attention, it will get stronger. But the good news is, if you feed the Good Wolf (the prefrontal cortex), it will get stronger.

Back to the public speaking, like I said, I was terrified when I started. I was so scared that I'd open my mouth and forget my own name! But then I trained my amygdala that speaking is *not* a threat. I kept doing it and doing it, leading with my prefrontal cortex until my amygdala got the message, "Hey, every time we do this, she lives through it. And she even feels pretty good afterwards."

I am still nervous about public speaking. It's not a "used to be" for me. I keep doing it. I get better each time (most of the time) but I don't feel like my heart is beating out of my chest and going to kill me through the entire talk. I feel nervous just for a few minutes until I relax (usually about 12 minutes). When I first started, my whole body said it was a life and death (probably death!) situation through my whole presentation. Now, the larger the crowd the more nervous I get, though it's starting to feel more like excitement than nervousness. Thankfully I pushed through because my ability to make an impact directly correlates to me being able to speak to and in front of people.

When you use the prefrontal cortex (Good Wolf), its neuropathways get stronger. But if you constantly respond to the fears and alarm signals of the amygdala (Bad Wolf), the amygdala gets stronger. So, when we stay stuck in our comfy ruts, don't take risks, stay fearful and doubtful or just complacent, those very same neuropathways become stronger. We become

> *The more we take risks, go after our dreams, challenge ourselves to go beyond what we thought we could do, get out of our comfort zone, try new things and venture out, the neuropathways to the prefrontal cortex become stronger.*

even *more* afraid of risks and stepping out of our comfort zone. The good news is that the opposite is true: The more we take risks, go after our dreams, challenge ourselves to go beyond what we thought we could do, get out of our comfort zone, try new things and venture out, the neuropathways to the prefrontal cortex become stronger. It becomes easier to take those leaps and bounds that help us grow so we can achieve our wildest dreams.

The point is that we need to get good at growing the prefrontal cortex neuropathways (Good Wolf) if we want the life we deserve. We don't want to totally *eliminate* the amygdala (Bad Wolf). We still want it to keep us from jumping off a bridge or running stark naked through downtown. But we want to pay less attention to it (which weakens it) so that it doesn't prevent us from asking that attractive person out, or making that sales call, or starting a new business or venture.

Unfortunately, many of us grew up feeding the Bad Wolf with all kinds of negative thoughts and beliefs that hold us back, things like

"I'm not very smart. I'll never succeed. I'll never be loved." The Bad Wolf responds to these beliefs and puts them down on its checklist of potential threats: "She's not smart, so no trying anything too complicated. Check. She'll never succeed so keep her away from trying to expand or trying anything new. Check. She'll never be loved so don't let her trust anyone. Check." These limiting beliefs are woven into our nervous systems, and they influence who we become and what we allow ourselves to do. By the time we're adults, the Bad Wolf has grown pretty darn powerful from all the fear and negativity we've fed it. So, it takes some real tenacity and persistence to weaken it.

But here's the good news: The Good Wolf, the one that wants us to thrive and be happy, never left the building even if we've ignored it, even if we never fed it any positive beliefs or uplifting thoughts. It's part of our DNA. It's like the instinct birds have to fly south in the winter. They'd probably survive if they didn't migrate but they'll only *thrive* if they fly south—and so they do. As humans, many of us have lost sight of the fact that we can literally create anything that we want in our lives, that we are meant to thrive, not just survive. We've lost sight of our Good Wolf. Thankfully, the Good Wolf is waiting very patiently inside to be recognized and fed. (For a video I did called the Good Wolf versus Bad Wolf visit KristaMashore.com/SSSBook)

Creating Change

> *"My new motto is: 'When you're through changing, you're through.'"*
> —*Martha Stewart*

So, I need to tell you honestly that changing from the Bad Wolf to the Good Wolf is simple, but it's not *easy*. Keep in mind that those negative thoughts and beliefs bouncing around your head are actually *wired* into your physiology. The limiting beliefs have built up a bunch of "evidence" over the years to prove that they're "true." That's because the RAS looked for "evidence" that supported those beliefs. So, they have a lot of history, energy and emotion behind them.

Think about that elephant. As a baby, it made a conscious connection: "I'm tied to the stake" so "I can't go free." It had a real experience of not being able to get free and after a few experiences, it became wired in. As it grew up and got bigger, it didn't get up every morning and have to consciously think the thought of "Yep, I'm still tied to that stake so I can't get free." Its *body* and *emotions* were telling it, "No use even trying." The elephant *knew for sure in every cell of its being* that it couldn't go free because that belief had been wired into its neurology and those neuropathways had become strong.

What about Mohini? In the beginning she may have thought (I'm pretty sure elephants and tigers think though maybe not in these exact words), "Huh. I'm in a cage and I can't go anywhere." Over the years, her body and emotions got used to being in that cage and used to not going anywhere. Maybe she even felt safer from all those crazy people who came to stare at her. Those neuropathways got really strong. When she finally got to her new environment that was open and free, she didn't just calmly think, "Huh. Maybe I'll just go hang out in that little corner instead." No! Her old neuropathways fired up and alerted everything in her body and emotions to get the heck out of the open space and back to some safe little corner! Being caged was *wired* into her nervous system.

Think about something that you *know* you shouldn't do but you keep doing it anyway, like eating too many fattening foods when you're trying to fit back into your jeans. You aren't just thinking, "Hey, a fourth bowl of Chunky Monkey would be nice right now." No! Your whole body is *craving* it. Emotionally, you might feel like you *need* it to feel better. The pattern in your brain is so strong that, despite being smart enough to know it's a bad idea and counter to your goal, you have the strong urge to do it.

Now think about something you know you *should* do or that you really *want* to do that you always find a way to avoid, for example, working out in the morning. If you have the mindset of "I hate this. It's going to be hard. I'd rather get a few more ZZZs," it's really tough to get yourself going. Your brain has notified your entire body and your emotions, "Hey, guys, this is *not* going to be fun" so they do their part and make you feel resistant and sluggish. Consciously, it's something you want to do but everything else in your system is saying, "No! Let's stay in bed!" You may force yourself out anyway but you're fighting yourself all the way. The good news is, the more you just do it, haul yourself out of bed and get to the gym, and the more you shift your negative thoughts about it, the easier it becomes because you've built that Good Wolf neuropathway.

That's why changing your mindset is not just saying one affirmation and—Boom!— you're done. Really shifting limiting beliefs means you need to do your synaptic pruning to get away from those negative thoughts and beliefs that have been running the show and keeping you caged. Then you need to feed the Good Wolf with thoughts and beliefs that will set you free. When you do this time and again, keep in mind that you're actually making physical changes to the way your nervous system processes. And that, my friends, takes consistency and persistency.

But you can do this! A while back, I was talking to a friend of mine, and she told me that the forests in the U.S. are moving. I was like, "Say what? Trees can't move." She said that about two-thirds of all forests are moving west and about half are moving north. It's in response to changing temperatures, wildfires, and less rain. So now I'm thinking, "Okay so they're plucking their little roots out of the ground and marching down the road?" But she explained that it's like having a line of ten people standing holding hands. We ask the guy on one end to let go and sit down. Then we ask another guy to join us on the *other* end. We do that often enough and the whole line has moved, right? What these forests are doing is allowing more trees to *die off on one end* while getting more young saplings to *grow on the other end* where climate conditions are better for them. Pretty smart, right? I mean it's amazing that trees know how to do that. They're just trees.

I only tell you this story because I'm pretty sure that you are at least as smart as a tree. If a forest can move and change to get what it wants, I know for sure that you can change your mindset to support what you want.

I really want you to follow your passions, go after your dreams and become the person you want to be. And you absolutely *can* do that if you get your mindset straight. Don't let yourself down, or you're going to look back with regret that you didn't even give it your best shot. I heard Dean Graziosi once give a great analogy: "What if at the end of your life, you walk up to your Maker and he says, 'Hey, let me show you a video of who you *could have been* if you'd just followed through.' How horrible would that be?!?" Honestly, that image alone could give you nightmares, right?

When people look back at their lives, they have the most remorse and the most regret and the most sorrow over things they know they *could* have done— and didn't. It's not the things you can't control that you'll regret the most. It's the *things that you have control over that you didn't take control of.* And your mindset is definitely one of those things that you CAN control.

> When people look back at their lives, they have the most remorse and the most regret and the most sorrow over things they know they could have done—and didn't.

Let's repeat that: Your mindset is *definitely* one of the things you can control.

It's All Up to You

In the long run, we shape our lives, and we shape ourselves. The process never ends until we die. And the choices we make are ultimately our own responsibility.
—*Eleanor Roosevelt*

I saw a punching bag in the gym that said, "There's nothing between you and the bag." I thought about that and realized that it's true about everything. There's nothing between you and your happiness. There's nothing between you and your finances. There's nothing between you and your relationship. There's nothing between you and your success. It's not your boss. It's not the environment. It's not the economy. It's not the interest rates. It's not your genetics. It's not your parents. It's all *you*. And until you come to the realization that nobody's coming to save you, you'll stay stuck.

We were all screwed up in life by the Cinderella stories where the prince saves the poor girl from poverty, or some magic sword saves the warrior in battle. We're waiting for the white knight or the magic to make it all better. We're waiting for a savior. But nobody's coming to save us. We have to take responsibility for the results we get in life.

All the results you get in life are on you. If you're a victim of rape, or child abuse or any of that kind of thing, obviously, I'm not saying *that* is on you. But you are responsible for how you choose to live your life after it.

You are the only one responsible for creating the life that you deserve. You do deserve it, but do you want it bad enough? Because no one is coming to save you and deliver it to you overnight. It's on you to make it happen. You have to realize that you are the creator of every single part of where you've landed and where you're going. Really, really stop right now and just hear me on this and take this in! I mean even forests have figured out that it's up to them!

Many times, I've heard of people who may have been defeated a lot or had a lot of rejection, so they just assume this mindset of "This is just the way it is. It's because of my parents. It's because the economy's bad. It's because my high school sweetheart cheated on me. It's because of the interest rates. It's because they cut me from the team." In their world, it's always somebody or something *else* between them and what they want.

Nope, there's nothing in the way. It's all you. You have the ability to do whatever you want. In fact, even during the COVID shutdowns, there were so many businesses that prospered. There were so many people who fell in love and got married. There were so many people who got their degrees or learned totally new skills. Many people went for what they wanted, and they got results because they took responsibility for making it happen. I wrote a book called *F.I.R.E., Financially Independent, Retire Early*. It's specifically for people who want to make a change and become their own boss but who have been held back by fear or limiting beliefs or just not knowing that it's a real possibility for them. The book makes it clear that they *can* make it happen.

I don't know what you believe, but personally, I feel it was our Creator that wired the Good Wolf instinct into all of us. Creator may not be a word you relate to. Maybe you think of a Universal Power or God or Infinite Intelligence or maybe you believe in none of that. That's okay. Don't let the words get in the way of the message. Insert your own words. The bottom line is that there is *something inside of all of us that wants us to succeed*. We were built to have what we desire in life, all to achieve our dreams and to thrive. We are no less than the birds with their natural instinct to fly south so they can thrive, or those forests that knew they had to move.

So, throughout this book we'll be building a great mindset that will support you in creating the life you desire and the success you want by doing lots of "synaptic pruning" of the Bad Wolf while feeding that Good Wolf everything it needs to become unstoppable!

Bad Wolf	Good Wolf
ANGRY	ABUNDANCE
BROKE	BOUNTIFUL BOLD
UNEASY	ULTIMATE
NEGATIVE	NEW
DOWN/TIRED	DISCIPLINED
ANXIETY/FEAR	AFFLUENT
NERVOUS/SCARED	NOBLE
CONTROL	CALM CAREFREE
EXCUSES	ENERGETIC ENTHUSIASTIC

Deadly Nightshade: Our Limiting Beliefs

"Beliefs have the power to create, and the power to destroy. Human beings have the awesome ability to take any experience of their lives, and create a meaning that disempowers them, or one that can literally save their lives."
—*Tony Robbins*

Earl Nightingale was a radio announcer and a motivational speaker in the 1950s. In 1956, he recorded a talk called *The Strangest Secret* on an actual vinyl record (anybody remember those?) and it sold more than a million copies! Here's how he described beliefs work in our brains:

"Suppose a farmer has some land, and it's good, fertile land. The land gives the farmer a choice; he may plant in that land whatever he chooses. The land doesn't care. It's up to the farmer to make the decision…Now, let's say that the farmer has two seeds in his hand—one is a seed of corn, the other is nightshade, a deadly poison. He digs two little holes in the earth and he plants both seeds—one corn, the other nightshade. … what will happen? Invariably, the land will return what was planted…Remember the land doesn't care. It will return poison in just as wonderful abundance as it will corn."[1]

Our brains are like super-fertile farmland. What you plant in it is what you get. And sometimes you get even *more* than you planted, and it doesn't matter whether it's poison or a great crop. A limiting belief-seed starts out as a tiny thought or doubt that grows until finally it gets really big and its roots are deep. If the seed you plant and feed is positive and makes you feel confident and empowered (Good

---

1   You can find audio versions of this talk and it was also put into a book.

Wolf, prefrontal cortex stuff), you'll naturally approach life that way. Challenges will still come up, but you'll know, "Hey. I got this." But if you plant deadly nightshade (Bad Wolf, amygdala thoughts), you'll naturally feel less capable, doubtful, hesitant and all kinds of rotten feelings. You'll fold when you hit problems. And the actions you try to take to succeed will be undermined by the poisonous beliefs you planted.

Henry Ford said, "Whether you think you can or think you can't, you're right!" If you *believe* that you can do something, if it's firmly planted, you can do it! You *know* you can do it so you act as if you can do it. You take risks, you step out of your comfort zone, you're willing to try things you've never tried before and keep going *because* you believe you'll succeed in the end.

And the flip side is true too: If you believe you *can't* do something, it will be nearly impossible to do it. You won't take the action you need to take, you'll hold back, you'll hide out under your blankie whenever you hit a big bump in the road. Why? Remember how your RAS (reticular activating system) is trying to please you and prove that you're right about things? When you *believe* you can't do something, it does everything in its power to make sure that you can't.

Your Bad Wolf amygdala gets into the act and sends warning signals to all of your systems. Sometimes it's subtle, like making you doubt yourself so that you don't persist. Other times, it's like a two by four that womps you over the head, making you physically sick or so terrified you can't breathe when you try to do something that your unconscious "knows for sure" you cannot do.

The thing about beliefs is that they seem *absolutely true* but they're often false! But because we believe them, they create *false obstacles and limitations*. Does it have to be that way? Nope. Here are some limiting beliefs that a lot of people would say are "true":

"Of course, I'm too short to play professional basketball. I'm only 5'11." If Spud Webb (who is 5'7") had believed that "truth," he would never have played in the NBA or won the NBA Slam Dunk contest.

"I'm too old to go back to college. I'm already forty." If Nola Ochs from Kansas had that belief, she never would have graduated from college at age ninety-five.

"I'm too young to make a difference." Alexa Grabelle didn't believe that and so she went ahead at age 10 and created the nonprofit Bags of Books that has distributed more than 120,000 children's books to kids who can't afford them in schools, homeless shelters and children's hospitals. Joshua Williams didn't believe it either so, at 8 years old, he founded Joshua's Heart, a nonprofit that has distributed more than 1.5 million pounds of food to over 350,000 people in South Florida, Jamaica, Africa, India and the Philippines.

Now think about it: What if these people had planted the deadly nightshade of those limited beliefs instead? What if they had *believed* what most people around them probably believed that they *couldn't* do what they did? They would have missed amazing opportunities and a ton of fulfillment in their lives. And the world would *not* have benefited from all the gifts they shared. It's the same with you and me. We may not join the NBA or start international non-profits before we're old enough to even get a drivers' license, but we *all* have unique gifts to offer that only *we* can give the world. We all can be more than our limiting beliefs tell us we are.

None of those supposedly "limitations" got in the way of people who *didn't believe* in them! The truth is that 99% of the limitations we think we have are just flat out lies we've told ourselves! They're just beliefs we absorbed and planted in our brains along the way. It doesn't really matter where or how you got them. The time you can break through them is now. And honestly, it doesn't even matter if your limiting beliefs are "true" or not. It's whether they support you and your goals and dreams. Let me repeat that:

It doesn't matter if your limiting beliefs are true or not. It's whether they support or undermine your dreams and goals in life.

> It doesn't matter if your limiting beliefs are true or not. It's whether they support or undermine your dreams and goals in life.

Tattoo that on your forehead. (Or, if that's too extreme for you, how about writing it with a sharpie on your forearm?)

We get these seeds of belief from all kinds of places. By the time we're seven, most of us have a ton of limiting beliefs, some from our parents, teachers, other kids, you name it. Little girls were told that they would never make great engineers. Little boys were told that "Boys don't cry." Often it's with the best intentions, like when your parents said, "Eat all of your food because there are starving kids in Africa." I'm guessing that one saying created a ton of eating disorders. A friend of mine had parents who told her that she should be part of the "Clean Plate Club," meaning she was supposed to eat all the food put in front of her. As a kid, she could never figure out why people liked going to restaurants because every time she went, she ended up with a tummy ache from eating so much food! How many people have gotten overweight following this advice?

We pick this stuff up all over the place. Sometimes we get them by comparing ourselves (or being compared) to other people. We can get a belief from little remarks someone makes in passing without even thinking about it, and we latch onto it like it's one of the Ten Commandments or something!

We gather and plant even more limiting beliefs as we get older and have experiences that we draw conclusions from. "I got a D in Algebra in 7th grade *so* that proves I'm no good with numbers." "He left me *so* obviously I'm not attractive enough or lovable enough." "That publisher rejected my manuscript *so* that proves I'm not talented enough to make it as a writer."

When I was little, my brother (who I always loved like crazy) used to call me Miss Piggy. I had a thing for Miss Piggy and I brought my Miss Piggy doll everywhere. But Miss Piggy had a really big nose and was chunky. So, when he called me that, I internalized it and thought it meant that I was fat and had a big nose. Every time I looked in a mirror, I would see this big nose. Every time I looked in the mirror, I saw my body as being on the larger side. We're all wired to come to a *conclusion* after something happens, but that isn't usually what it meant at all. It's just what we decided it meant—and it can be deadly nightshade. The Bad Wolf amygdala *loves* to feed on poisonous conclusions like this, and they make it stronger!

With my history of being abused, I ended up with a *ton* of negative beliefs about myself: "I'm not worthy. I'll never be loved. I'm not good enough. Nobody likes me." Your limiting beliefs might not be as heavy, but we've *all* got them. "I'm not smart enough/handsome enough/

athletic enough/talented enough/strong enough." Just fill in your own blanks.

You might say, "No, Krista, this one is *real.* I really don't have the money to do this thing." "I really don't have the time to get everything done." "I really don't have the right degree." "I really am too weak/too shy/too cowardly." Trust me, I've heard them all! And they are all BS! That deadly nightshade your Bad Wolf has been bingeing on makes it *feel* like a *real* limitation but it's not. Which of these sad stories or others are you telling yourself? When I hear sad stories like this, I just want to yell, "JUST STOP IT!!! You have so much more that you could be or do in your life if you just QUIT telling yourselves those stories!"

But even if you know intellectually they aren't real, limiting beliefs are still a big issue for most of us. Remember that they're planted, wired into your neurology so they don't just abracadabra presto disappear. Unfortunately, I can't just leap out of this book and yank that deadly nightshade out of your system! I can't swoop in and muzzle that Bad Wolf for you. You're the only one who can do it. You have to stop feeding the Bad Wolf and piling other negative stories on top of the negative belief you've already got planted in there. If you don't then you're choosing to buy into the Bad Wolf and live the limited, mediocre life that you never wanted to live. The life of your nightmares, not your dreams.

Because remember, these beliefs are planted in our neurology, and they cause us to *take action* or *avoid taking action* and our actions determine our results in life. If we don't believe in ourselves, we're hesitant, afraid to put ourselves out there, afraid to be different. We're afraid to go for it. All because of a bunch of self-limiting beliefs. *These beliefs aren't who we really are, but we act as if they are.*

Your limiting beliefs are not just quiet little thoughts that roam around in your head, not causing any trouble. No, a limiting belief will activate your nervous system and trigger your emotions. It will make you want to act in ways that do *not* serve you. Remember the elephant and Mohini? Your whole system gets into the belief. You won't start that business. You won't ask that attractive person out for a date. You won't submit your sculpture to that contest. You won't apply for that job or program. You won't try out for the team. Your limiting beliefs will have you heading in the absolute *opposite* direction from your dreams. Your beliefs about yourself—deadly nightshade or tasty, nutritious corn— are a *major* part of your overall mindset, I'd say about 95% of it. They either boost you toward what you want or keep you in your little cage.

Let me give you a personal example: Years ago, I signed up for a super-expensive Master Mind group. I walked in and found this incredibly high-powered, talented, successful group of people and immediately I thought, "I'm way out of my league!" It's not that I hadn't been successful. I was already in the Top 1% of Producers in real estate nationally. But these people were the rock stars of training and coaching. I was just a newbie still trying to figure it all out. My palms got sweaty, my heart started pounding and I felt panicked. When I had to speak at that first meeting, I felt inferior. I was so nervous about saying the wrong thing or looking stupid. When the words finally came out, I felt like my heart was going to literally burst out of my chest. But I'd been working on my mindset. I had a crystal-clear vision and strong sense of purpose, and I had convinced myself (almost) that I was worthy of this dream that I had to coach and train people. I knew I had to get out of my comfort zone for that to happen. I was savvy enough to recognize a limiting belief when I heard one like, "I'm way out of my league!" I also knew what to do about it.

So, I took a deep breath, shook myself off and I changed what I was saying to myself. I stopped adding fertilizer to that deadly nightshade by saying "Why are you here? You don't belong here. You can never accomplish what these people have, what are you thinking." Instead, I used the Stop, Snap and Switch to get out of my negative thinking. I planted better seeds: "If these people can do this, so can I. They are not better or worse than me. And I'm going to knock this out of the park!"

And thank goodness I stayed and changed my self-talk, because just 4 years later, I was making more of an impact and more financially than most of the people who were in that room. Because I stayed in that group—and kept working on strengthening my mindset—I was able to build a multi-million-dollar coaching business in under a year. If I'd walked out of that room because I didn't feel "good enough", I never could have done that. And I wouldn't have written this book and you wouldn't be reading this book (which by the way I hope is making an impact on you).

That mastermind team and being in the room with those great people absolutely helped shape and build my business and really my life.

To build my coaching business, did I have to work to improve my skills? Yes. Did I soak up learning to increase my knowledge? Absolutely. Did I work like crazy to make it happen? You betcha. But mindset is *always* more important than skill set. Without the burning desire, confidence and *belief that I could do what it takes,* none of that knowledge or those skills or even the hard work would have mattered one bit. I would have retreated back into my comfy comfort zone at the first sign of trouble when things got tough. I would have doubted myself and avoided taking risks or making decisions.

My main goal now is to get people to believe in themselves. They need to believe that I'm not a unicorn and I'm not some superhuman. I'm not an exception, I'm an example. I share my personal story so you know, "Hey, if Krista can do it, I can do it." I mean, really, I had some of the crappiest limiting beliefs anybody could have! But I realized how important it was to get rid of them if I had any chance of creating the life I wanted. So, I worked really hard to change them.

Great beliefs that support who we want to be are not something most of us were born with. A great, positive mindset is definitely not something I was born with. But like all the success principles that Napoleon Hill teaches, they can be *learned.* I had to work on this muscle constantly, and I still have to work on it constantly. I'm to the point in my life now where there's *nothing* that I think I can't do. I mean I know I can't fly (although that would be really cool), and I can't suddenly disappear (that would be awesome too) into thin air. But I feel like I can do anything that others have shown to be possible, and that I really want and that I commit my focus to.

How do we even know what's possible or not? Less than 100 years ago, people would have said that flying to the moon or instantly sending a photo to people all over the world was impossible. Now we think nothing about talking to someone on your phone with a video on. I remember watching the George Jetson cartoons. As a kid, I was mesmerized that they could talk on the phone and see each other on the phone or T.V. It seemed so unreal and impossible. Now we do it all the time without even thinking about how amazing it really is!

I really believe that you can just do anything that you put your mind to as well. It's all about truly believing that you can get what you want in life if you really go for it. You can't build that belief and still carry around a bunch of crummy limiting beliefs. You've got to replace the poison and plant the good stuff.

It's not just getting all fired up one day then going back to your same old same old routines and habits. You can't just plant a few seeds and call it good. You have to keep weeding out the poisonous thoughts and beliefs, then watering and giving good fertilizer to the positive ones. You need to make sure your positive plants get the right environment (and we'll talk about how to do all this throughout the book).

It's like getting into physical shape. It doesn't just happen by working out in the gym one day, especially if you're in rotten shape to begin with. It takes tenacity and persistence and doing specific exercises consistently that will get your mindset where you need to be. Often you need a coach, and it really helps to have a support group as you train.

Training yourself to believe in yourself is the same thing. You might feel motivated by just reading this book, but it won't change anything unless you *apply* it consistently and persistently. You need to incorporate the practices and exercises into *your daily routine*. You need to immerse yourself in becoming the person you want to be and pay really close attention to what you're planting in your brain. You need to realize that having beliefs about yourself that will support your success is more important than all the specific skills and strategies in the world. It's more important than any dating advice or business coaching. It's more important than parenting classes or practicing your sport. I know, that sounds crazy but it's true.

You also need to realize that having a rotten mindset where you *don't* believe in yourself is a guarantee for not achieving what you want.

Okay, so how do you uproot those poisonous beliefs? First, you have to be aware of them *and the damage they're doing to you*. Then you need to come up with a new belief that will support where you want to go. This exercise will get you started.

Uprooting Poisonous Beliefs

"Life is way too short to spend another day at war with yourself."
—*Dean Grazioso*

Take out a sheet of paper and write down all—I mean *all*—of the limiting beliefs you have about yourself. Remember, the Bad Wolf will trick you into *feeling certain* that some of them are really real! Write them down anyway. Think about times in the past when you started to go for something but then backed off or something mean that you say to yourself about yourself that you would *never* say to a friend! Even if you know consciously that it isn't true, if it pops up every once in a while and zaps your confidence, write it down anyway. Some of those negative things you say to yourself may seem really tiny, like they wouldn't really make a difference. Write them down anyway.

Now think about situations where you feel uncomfortable. Do you have some belief about yourself that makes you feel that way? Think about something you would love to do but never have. What's the belief about yourself that kept you from doing it? What don't you have in your life that you wish you could have? What's the reason (excuse) for why you don't have it? What would you like to be that you aren't being? What's stopping you? Write down that one (Unless it's "being 20 years younger"! Not going to happen!)

When you've got your list, stop and think about a belief for each one that would be more empowering. For example, if it's "I'm just not good with money", you might write down, "I'm great at managing my money and getting better all the time." You probably don't want to start with "I'm a financial genius!" because your Bad Wolf will just laugh at you! Or say your belief is, "I'm too old to change careers now. I'll just ride it out." You can switch it out to "With the wisdom and experience I've gained, now is the perfect time to make a career change." Start with something you can believe or almost believe, something that will shift how you feel about money.

When you've finished your lists, I recommend that my students put the new positive beliefs on sticky notes all around the house so they can see them constantly. For the old beliefs, a lot of people like to tear them up and even stomp on them! (To see a video where you can watch some of them do it go to KristaMashore.com/SSSBook and find the video called Getting Free of Negative Beliefs.) You can even do a little ritual of burning them—just make sure you don't burn the house down! Getting some support in shifting your beliefs is super important. So, join the Facebook group http://www.facebook.com/groups/stopsnapandswitch here and post your new beliefs so others can root for you! And post a video if you want of yourself tearing up those limiting beliefs or burning them away to help inspire others.

Was it helpful to uproot your negative beliefs and start planting new positive ones? If so, help me help others by leaving a review about my book on Amazon. Thank you!

Next, start using Stop, Snap and Switch whenever these negative beliefs pop up. Whenever you hear that negative belief creep in, stop, snap your wristband, and switch it to the other hand as you say the new belief. You may not catch them all at first but soon you'll find yourself super-aware of them. Be sure to replace the negative belief with your new, improved positive one. (If you can't remember exactly, don't worry about it. Just come up with something in the moment that works for you.)

The Stories
That Cage Us

"I have known many sorrows, most of which never happened."
—*Mark Twain*

Have you heard the story about the little boys who woke up on Christmas morning and found a pile of horse manure rather than toys under their tree? The first little boy started to cry and throw a tantrum. "We aren't going to have any Christmas. This is the worst day of my life. I must have done something terrible for Santa to give me poop for Christmas!" The second little boy laughed and started shoveling the manure like crazy saying, "With all this manure, there just got to be a pony in here somewhere!" That's definitely an optimistic kid with a great mindset, right?

The point is that he looked at the same *facts* as the other kid and, rather than interpreting them to mean that Santa thought he was a bad boy or that Christmas was going to be awful (which I think most people would think), he looked at that pile of poop, and decided it meant something great was coming! The first little boy had the same *facts* but came to a totally different conclusion about it, a conclusion that made him miserable about himself and about Christmas. Which one was "right?" It doesn't really matter. Remember, it's whether that belief or that conclusion or that story supports our dreams and goals or not.

We all do this every single day of our lives! Something happens and—Bam!—we come up with an interpretation and make up a story about it. "That guy cut me off. He must be a jerk!" "That client isn't calling back. They must hate my work, or maybe they hired someone else!" "My kid isn't doing well in school. He's not very bright or maybe I'm a bad parent." It happens so fast! To get a stronger mindset, you have to begin paying attention to the difference between the *facts* of a situation and the *story* you tell yourself about that situation. Fact: A guy cut you off. You have no idea why he did it or who he is. He might be racing to the hospital because his kid got hit by a car. Fact: Your client hasn't called. You have no idea why or what's going on in their lives. Fact: Your kid isn't doing well in school. You have no idea if it has anything to do with their intelligence or your parenting. Everything you say after stating the facts is just fiction!

There's a huge and very critical difference between those two. The *facts* are just what happened in the past or what is happening now. Our *stories* are the conclusions, interpretations and the meanings we give to the facts. We base them on our beliefs. So, for the two little boys at Christmas, one probably believed something like, "Life is tough and it's hard to get what you want." The little boy with the shovel probably believed something like, "Life always gives me good stuff. I just need to find it and work for it!" Can you see how those different beliefs would affect how they'd approach *everything* in their lives?

Often people hold such strong beliefs in their heads that they don't even *see* the facts at all! We all think we're being objective but we're not. Psychologist Dennis Proffitt and Drake Baer wrote a book called *Perception: How Our Bodies Shape Our Minds*. They had done a bunch of studies on perception versus reality. One showed that people who were obese or out of shape saw distances literally as *farther* than they really were. I'm guessing they had some belief that "walking distances is difficult" so distances that they might have to walk looked farther to them. In another experiment, they took a bunch of hikers. Some didn't carry anything, and others got heavy backpacks to carry. The ones with the heavy backpacks saw the hills in front of them as *much steeper* than the people who didn't wear a backpack. The *facts* were exactly the same, but they saw them differently.

You also *only see the facts that fit with what you believe*. Have you ever shared an old memory with a family member about something that happened in the past, only to find out that your memories of that event were *totally different*? "Mom wasn't mad at us that day. She never got mad." "We never got good presents from Aunt Betty. She hated us." You each have different beliefs so what your brain "remembered" was filtered by those beliefs. When this happens, don't you feel absolutely positive that *your* story is the right one and theirs is wrong? I'm telling you, you *cannot* trust everything you think. The stories we tell ourselves about the past and the present are just made-up fantasies based on our beliefs. They're not just the "facts." The facts have been filtered through our beliefs and how we see the world.

Let me give you an example: Take two kids who went to the summer county fair one year. Twenty years later, they sit around reminiscing about growing up and that day at the fair comes up. One of them says, "Yeah, it was so cool! There were all these beautiful animals everywhere. We got to eat those great corn dogs and have cotton candy. And that house of mirrors was awesome!" The other person looks at him and says, "Are you kidding me? That was the worst day ever. It was hot as blazes, and I got a sunburn. The whole place stunk like manure. That cheap corn dog was greasy and made me sick, and I ended up all sticky from the cotton candy. That stupid house of mirrors was just crowded and stuffy and I couldn't wait to get out of there!" So, which one has the facts? Well, probably both of them. But can you see how their individual perspectives made their experiences of that day totally different? One clearly remembers going to a "hot, stinky, crummy" fair where the other clearly remembers a terrific day. It's not the facts of the situation that make the biggest difference. It's the story you hang on to about it.

It's not that facts don't matter, but the *stories* we tell about them are much more important. The facts are just the facts. Think about it. Don't you know some people who grew up with great family support, who had loving parents, and who were provided a great education, yet they still failed? Even though they were born with a silver spoon in their mouth, they still lived their whole life being miserable, hating their jobs, unhappy in their relationships, and being physically unhealthy.

And you probably know other people who had horrendous childhoods, maybe who were abused emotionally or physically. Or people who had very little in terms of resources or money as they grew up and maybe no education at all. You would think that those people would be the ones most likely to fail. Yet, many of the people we most admire who have achieved incredible success in all areas and who are happy and fulfilled actually started out that way. The Oprah Winfrey's of the world, people like Eminem and Jay-Z, Mahatma Gandhi and Abraham

Lincoln. So here is what I want you to understand and to really hear me: Your success has nothing to do with your biography. It has nothing to do with the facts of your background.

It's our *stories about these facts* that can make or break us. They start out being based on our beliefs and then those stories *strengthen* the same beliefs they were built from, either positive or negative, every single time we tell it. Those beliefs and stories lead to our actions which lead to results we get in life. We can tell ourselves stories that make us feel down and hopeless like the first little boy at Christmas, or we can tell ourselves stories that make us feel awesome and unstoppable like the second kid who pulled out his shovel! You can almost predict how those two lives are going to turn out, can't you?

The Buddhists say that all of our suffering comes from our thoughts. I don't think they're saying that we don't have painful or difficult facts we've got to face. They're saying that our *real suffering comes from the stories we tell ourselves—and keep telling ourselves— about those difficult facts.* Look, the facts of my childhood are just the facts. But I made the choice to rewrite my story about it so that I didn't keep suffering.

I heard an old Taoist story about a farmer. He had a horse who pulled his plow when he worked his crops. One day, his horse ran away. His neighbors all shook their heads and said, "What rotten luck!" The farmer just shrugged and said, "Maybe." The next morning his horse came back and was followed by three beautiful wild horses. His neighbors congratulated the farmer on his great luck. The farmer shrugged and said, "Maybe."

The next day, his son tried to ride one of the wild horses. It bucked him off and he broke his leg. The neighbors came by and said, "How awful!" but the farmer just shrugged and said, "Maybe." A week or so after the accident, army officers came into the village. They were there to draft all the young men into the army to go to war. Because the son had a broken leg, they didn't draft him. The neighbors congratulated the farmer on how well things had turned out. Like always, he just shrugged and said, "Maybe."

When people hear about the story of my childhood, they'll say, "Oh, Krista, how horrible!" And I tell them that I totally disagree. First of all, and I know it sounds crazy, but my family was really very loving and we had a lot of good times. It was like I was living two lives: One was being in this very happy, loving family and the other was experiencing the abuse from my mom. And, yes that part was very tough at the time, but if it hadn't happened, I know I would not be who I am today. I know I would not be able to make the impact that I'm making. Telling my story has helped people come out of the woodwork and say how much the story helped them through some roadblocks.

When my mom had that meltdown, telling me how sorry she is, that she feels so much guilt, she sobbed for an hour and a half. My mom had a horrible childhood. When I was born it triggered something in her, and that was part of the reason for the abuse. So, I said to her, "First of all, you're an amazing mother because when I came to you, you went to counseling with me. You owned up to it. You helped me heal, and you told dad. And because of what happened, it's made me a fighter. I kick butt in life. If it hadn't happened, I wouldn't be able to help people like I'm doing."

In the bible, there's a story about Joseph whose brothers sold him into slavery when he was a teenager. (Talk about having it rough in your adolescence! I'm thinking that being sold as a slave was much worse than not getting asked to prom or getting cut from the basketball team!) Joseph had some other problems along the way (like getting thrown into prison for something he didn't do) but eventually, he became a powerful governor of Egypt and saved the country from a famine. When his brothers showed up one day, he looked at them and said, "As for you, what you intended against me for evil, God intended for good, in order to accomplish a day like this— to preserve the lives of many people." Now *that's* a powerful story about a pretty horrible situation! But what story could he have come up with? He could have felt unworthy because his brothers turned against him. He could have decided that there was nothing for him to do but keep his head down and be a good slave. He could have continued hating not only his brothers but all the Egyptians who kept him as a slave. He chose to tell a much better story.

We can't change the facts, folks. But we can always change our stories about them. So, what kinds of stories are you telling yourself right now? Are you telling yourself stories that are causing you pain and suffering? Or are your stories helping you look for the pony? The stories you tell yourself right now will not only affect your mood and mindset. They will definitely affect your actions and your results.

I look back at the situation with my former husband. We had a pretty rough divorce and when he left, it was horrible. I thought things were going to be terrible for me and my daughters. But I look back now and I know it was the best thing that could have happened. If it hadn't, I wouldn't be with my husband, Steve, who is awesome! He's my best friend and the love of my life! I'd probably be in jail for murdering my ex or I'd be dead, because that's how bad it was getting. I would never have had the confidence and the happiness to be able to coach people. But now that I'm with Steve, I've truly found a real partner, who makes me feel loved and accepted for who I am. Of course, we're normal and we have our issues. 96% of the time it's great. But there's 4% where he drives me nuts! But I could not be happier, and I could not feel more safe and secure because I'm now loved by such a loyal person. When I look back, I think, "Thank goodness that ugly divorce happened!"

I'm sure most of us have gone through breaking up with someone we were in love with. It's tough, right? But it's the *story* we tell ourselves that can keep us feeling miserable about it. If we tell ourselves, "This means I'm not lovable" or "This means I'll never find someone to love again" or "This means I'll die alone and lonely." Those *stories* we tell about it are what keep us in pain, not the fact that we got dumped. But what if we told ourselves, "That must mean that he or she wasn't the right one for me and there's someone else out there who is perfect for me just around the corner!" We'll still feel some pain, right? But we'd also feel empowered and hopeful and ready to get out there again! I truly believe that *every* painful story can be turned around like this if we choose to.

There are times when life does hand us a pile of poop: The economy tanks, a loved one dies, we get a horrible diagnosis, someone betrays us, yada yada yada. The facts of life hurt sometimes. But if the story we keep telling ourselves is, "I'll never be able to bring back my business or recoup my losses" or "I'll always be lonely" or "My life's over" or "I'll never trust anyone again," we're adding to the pain, *and* setting ourselves up for making those stories come true. We're strengthening our negative beliefs.

But if we interpret it differently, we'll have different results. Like that second little boy, when we can tell a different story and interpret the poop as, "Okay, so something good has to come from this. I wonder what it is? What can I do to find it?" Now we're focused on figuring out how things could be better in the future. We're looking for possibilities and maybe the lessons we could learn. We're not making ourselves suffer. We're looking for the pony.

Whatever has happened to you in your life has happened, right? But the way you *think* about it and *feel* about it *doesn't have to stay the same.* Like that farmer, things that looked bad at the time aren't necessarily bad. Like the kid with the poopy Christmas, you can dig for the treasure.

A friend of mine was doing a gratitude practice and flashed on the time she was in the hospital recovering from neck surgery and miserable from the morphine they were giving her. But what she remembered this time that she'd almost forgotten was that her sister had flown in to help her. Now, her sister was kind of a pain in the butt, but my friend realized that her sister had made the effort to fly across the country to be there for her, to support her. And suddenly, she wasn't focused on the icky morphine or the pain. She just felt loved and really grateful to her sister. It turned a stinky story into a positive one.

When things in our life happen, we have to just remind ourselves that, like that farmer, we *don't really know if it's bad or good in the long run.* Whether they're bad or good or indifferent, you don't really know what the outcome is going to be. We have to train ourselves to make our own outcomes. We have to train ourselves to tell stories about what happens that make us feel stronger and more capable. There's *always* a way to find something good out of every bad thing that happens. We have that choice.

Another friend of mine lost her only son. I can't even imagine losing a child and I'd definitely have a hard time finding anything good about it. But my friend said to me, "At a certain point, I realized that I had choice and I could make decisions. One of them was that I decided not to let my grief ruin all my happy memories with my son. I was going to go ahead and grieve, I'd let it have its way with me and get really messy weeping sometimes. But then when I have the happy memories, I got to have the happy memories. I decided to keep all of his photos up so I could think of him and those happy memories. Another decision I made was that I was going to tell people about it rather than just say 'no' if someone asked me if I had kids. It wasn't always easy, but when I answered honestly that, 'yes, I'd lost a son,' I found out that a lot of other people have lost children. They really appreciated that they could talk to me about it."

We can choose to shift the meaning of something from the past and also about things that are happening in the present. For example, I remember the very first days when the Covid pandemic first hit us. Honestly, part of me was freaked out and a little panicked. After I calmed myself down, I made the decision about who and what I wanted to be during that time. I started telling a different story. I decided I wanted to be a leader. I wanted to be an uplifter. I wanted to offer whatever I could during that time to help people out. So instead of hiding out on the couch and watching *I Love Lucy* reruns or ripping my hair extensions out and worrying about my business, I created a free 30-day series of video blogs with tips on how to stay positive and motivated. My intention to be a leader and uplifter during that time helped me stay focused and proactive through all of it.

Rewriting Your Personal Story

Rewriting your story to strengthen your mindset is about *rewriting the lesson or meaning you got from it.*
Go back to different difficult situations in your life and think about how you tell that story to yourself or to others. If it's

> Rewriting your story to strengthen your mindset is about rewriting the lesson or meaning you got from it.

positive, great! If not, ask yourself, "Okay, so what are some of the good things that happened from it or even during it? What lessons did I learn from it that have made me stronger or more loving or wiser?" Write down all the lessons and good stuff you didn't include in that old version of your story. When you think of a situation that seemed so horrible at the time and ask the question, "What good was in it?" it changes the meaning of that situation for you in the present. We remember it differently and it uplifts us rather than making us angry or sad or like a victim.

The second part of this is, of course, to catch yourself during the day whenever you start telling that moldy old negative story to yourself or someone else and Stop, Snap, and Switch. Stop and recognize that you've had a negative thought, snap your wristband and as you switch it to the other wrist, think about your new story with all the lessons and good stuff that came to you because of what happened.

Rewriting Your Global Stories

Not all of our global beliefs have a huge impact on our lives. Some, like "the weather in Chicago is always crummy" really don't matter much if you aren't heading to Chicago. Think of the global stories you tell yourself that *do* impact you. Start with "Life is…" and fill in the blank. When you have a list of those, use "People are…" and fill in the blank.

When you have a decent list, try this process from Byron Katie that I've paraphrased and added to:

First ask yourself: Is this story true? (If it's a strong belief and a story you've told over and over, you'll probably answer "Yes!")

Next ask: Can you absolutely know that this belief is true? (Okay, unless you're God or the Source of All Wisdom, you probably have to answer "no." You may have gathered "evidence" that it's true if your belief in the story is strong. But the bar for "absolutely true" is pretty high!)

Third, ask yourself: When you tell yourself that story, how do you feel? How do you act? What is it costing you? Remember that your beliefs determine your actions which determine your results! For example, if you think "Life is difficult," you may be struggling in everything you do!

Last question: Who would you be without that thought? What would you do that maybe you aren't doing now? How would you feel?

Sometimes just doing this process will help you get rid of a global belief that is holding you back. But if it pops up again, use your Stop, Snap and Switch process to nip it in the bud. Remember, we're working on synaptic pruning, so we want to make sure we don't keep heading down the neuropathway of the old story we want to be rid of!

Stories We Create About Others

If you change the way you look at things, the things you look at change.
—*Wayne Dyer*

Some of the stories we tell ourselves have to do with our beliefs about ourselves and some are about assumptions we make about things outside ourselves. Our assumptions are based on our limiting beliefs and the meaning we've given to our past happenings, just like our personal stories. Though we make up stories about all kinds of things, it's our assumptions about other people in our lives—what they are thinking, how trustworthy they are, how smart or capable they are, etc. etc—that mess us up the most. We take a few facts, (usually not very many!) and make them into a full-blown 500-page novel about that person! Our assumptions and stories about other people cause us to act differently toward them and even cause *them* to act differently. Let me repeat that:

Our assumptions and stories about other people cause us to act differently toward them and even cause *them* to act differently.

Years ago, there were a bunch of studies done with schoolchildren. A researcher would tell their teachers, "Okay,

> Our assumptions and stories about other people cause us to act differently toward them and even cause them to act differently.

these students are the smart students, and those others are the underachievers." The truth was that the two groups were chosen at random. The kids in the "slow" group were no more or less intelligent than the kids in the "smart" group. But by the end of the school year, the kids in the so-called smart group way outperformed the kids in the "slow" group. Their teacher's attitude toward them because of the story she'd been told had actually shaped the kids' behavior and results!

This isn't only true of students. Researchers have done a number of studies on leadership styles in the workplace. They reported that "empowering leaders," leaders who respect their employees, trust them with responsibility, and appreciate their efforts, end up with teams that were much more creative, motivated about their work, and higher performing. Basically, these leaders are telling themselves the story that their employees are fully capable and trustworthy. And so, the employees show up that way! The opposite was true of autocratic leaders. Autocratic leaders come across as "I'm the smartest guy in the room and you can't be trusted to do a good job." Their employees respond to this attitude and *that* story becomes true too!

Think about this in your personal life. The story you tell yourself about your spouse, kids or friends directly impacts how you treat them and how they respond! It's just like with anybody in your life, but you always have a greater impact on the people who are close to you. If you believe your kids are geniuses (even if that genius is pretty much hidden under some pretty not-so-smart behavior!), they'll start acting that way and have confidence in themselves. If you believe your spouse is the hottest thing walking planet earth, they'll start responding that way. If you believe that your friends are totally fun to be around, they'll start being more fun. And, of course, the *opposite* is true, too! If you walk around believing negative things about the people in your life, they'll respond to those negative messages as well, even if you never say them out loud.

Another area where we tend to make up a lot of stories about people is in *assuming we know what someone else is thinking or their intentions*. Say, a friend doesn't call you back. What's your very first assumption? "Maybe they're mad at me. Maybe I said something wrong. Maybe they don't really like me." Blah, blah, blah. We make up whole soap operas based on a look someone gives us or a tiny comment.

The truth is we don't know what's going on with other people. You can't know if a co-worker is cranky because they're dealing with a cheating spouse or a sick child. You don't know if your spouse is feeling guilty and bummed out because they wanted to give you a great anniversary present and couldn't find one or couldn't afford to buy you what they really wanted to. You don't know if your kids are grouchy and ornery because they're being bullied at school or got a bad grade on a test they worked hard for. We just don't know what's happening in other people's lives or in their heads. None of us have magic crystal balls. We need to learn to give others the benefit of the doubt and stop making up stories about *why* they did or said what they did. We may *think* we know but we never really do know. We're not in their heads and the stories we make up are a waste of time.

We also tend to take things way too personally. Isn't it weird how we think the world revolves around us? If your spouse is having a bad day, you think it's something *you* did or didn't do. If a client doesn't return your email, you think they're upset with you and your work. If your boss is in a bad mood, you think you're about to get fired or they don't like you.

Listen, 99% of the time, people's reactions have absolutely nothing to do with you! Think about it. If you're under financial pressure and you snap at the dog, does it really have anything to do with the dog? No. It has to do with what you're dealing with, not good old Fido. (And Fido is smart enough not to take it personally!) So, stop trying to be a mind reader and making up big stories about what's in other people's heads! Just Stop, Snap and Switch yourself right out of it!!!!

Another assumption we often make is that *others are just like us*. We all know (I hope!) that it *never* helps to compare ourselves to others, right? Well, it's just as destructive to compare *others* to *ourselves*. Here's a good one: "If he really loved me, he would help around the house more." That's a horrible story to tell yourself in so many ways! When you assume things like that, you're comparing him to what *you* would do to show love and caring. Your story says, "He *knows* how important it is to me that he helps out more. He just doesn't care enough about me!" Okay, how does that story make you feel? Resentful? Unloved? Unappreciated? What do you do with that story? Well, if you take that "he doesn't love me enough" far enough, you probably end up in divorce court!

Or how about, "If she really cared about this job, she would have gotten that project done faster no matter what." You're basing that assumption on what *you* would do. Maybe she's determined to get it right, or for some reason this project, which would have been easy for you, was particularly hard for her. You do not know why she didn't get it done faster, but your story about it can lead to wrecking your working relationship.

Here's one of the absolutely worst assumptions, *"They should know."* "My kids should know not to bother me when I'm on a call." "My staff should know to be on time for our meetings." "My spouse should know that I want to spend more time with him." Or "My friends should know that I said 'no' to wine night because I have a work deadline." No, folks, they don't know! You're not a mind reader and the people around you are not mind readers either! If the story you're telling yourself is that "they should just know," you'll be constantly disappointed, guaranteed! Just Stop, Snap and Switch yourself right out of those negative stories that don't have any validity to them.

Rewriting Stories About Other People

Here's another great opportunity to use your Stop, Snap and Switch. Start with just one person close to you and make a list of all the stories you tell yourself about that person. Maybe it's a belief about who they are or maybe it's an assumption about what they're thinking or feeling. Write it down. Ask yourself, "What does this belief make me feel about them? What are some of the ways I treat them or interact with them that are based on this story? Is this something that is positive for either of us?" If not, think of a new story you could tell yourself. Next, think about how you might change your behavior toward them based on this new story. What would you do differently? How would you act differently?

Then you know what to do: Whenever that old story pops up or you start treating that person in the old way, Stop, Snap and Switch!

Global Beliefs

The beliefs we have about ourselves and the people in our lives are extremely powerful. But the basic beliefs we have about life in general and people overall can also make a huge impact on us—positive or negative. I've heard these called "global beliefs" because they aren't about any particular other person, but they cover just about *all* people. They aren't about a specific situation, they pretty much cover *all* situations. Often, these global beliefs are shared by a bunch or even the majority of people. So, they may seem even truer because so many people have bought into them. But they're still just beliefs, not truths! Remember, our beliefs—whether it's about who you are or about how the world works and how other people are in general—will determine our actions which determine our results. So, just like your beliefs about yourself, you need to figure out which of these global beliefs are supporting you and which are holding you back. Let me give you some examples:

So maybe you're someone who tends to be distrusting. Perhaps you had a bad experience, and so you used that disappointment to create a broad assumption about people in general. Maybe your story says that people are always taking advantage of you. Maybe your story says that people are lazy, mean, greedy, selfish. With that kind of story going on in your head, every time you meet someone, you're on guard. You're just waiting for them to misuse the tiny bit of trust you give them. Before you even know them, you just *know* they're scheming about how to take advantage of you! Think about it. What kinds of relationships can you have in your personal and professional life with this crummy story running the show? Or does this global belief keep you from even having any relationships at all?!?

Your global beliefs about people will sound like "People are…" or "Kids are…" or "Men or Women are…" Just fill in the blank. It could be about certain groups like politicians or people from other countries or people in certain religions or ethnicities or cultures. It's a story you believe about a big group of people, and it impacts how you live your life! If it's positive like "Everyone is on my side!" you'll act as if clients will want to work with you, your boss is always trying to help you, your spouse is eager to support your dreams and goals—and the people in your life will respond to that story. If it's negative like "Women are all users," you'll avoid hiring women, you won't get close personally with them, you may even accuse women in your life of doing things they've never done. Basically, your chance of good relationships with women is doomed! (In fact, if you're a woman yourself, this belief can even impact the relationship you have with yourself!)

We often also have stories we make up about people who are highly successful. We assume that they were born into wealth, or they are genetically predisposed to be a great athlete or amazing in business. We believe that they were naturally outgoing and enthusiastic, so things were easier for them. None of that is true. The truth is many people who are super successful come from *very* difficult backgrounds (parts of my background for example). Like me, those successful people may look as though they've just "got it going on" so to speak. But now you know that I'm the girl who hasn't lived at home since I was 13, who couldn't read and wet the bed. Our false stories about people and their success are only giving us excuses as to why *we* are *not* successful and doing the things they do. Like most other assumptions, that type of thinking is just false and only holds you back. Like other limiting beliefs, it will cause you to think, feel and act in ways that don't serve you.

Global beliefs and stories can also be about how life works. "Life is not fair" or "Life is so hard" or "Life is just a bowl of cherries!" Global beliefs and stories like these become your basic philosophy. Are they true? Who knows? What I do know is that the stories you tell about the way life works can make you feel supported or totally overwhelmed!

How about this global belief about life: "In life, external circumstances determine my outcomes and my life." I've got to tell you that a heck of a lot of people would agree with that one! They live their lives just waiting for the next shoe to drop. They feel like victims of whatever way the wind blows. No matter what kind of hand they get dealt, they figure it's all about luck, not how they play their cards. But that's false. In *any* circumstance, even the seemingly worst ones, you can always find someone who found a way to turn it around for themselves. For example:

The economy: This is a biggie for many folks. "The economy is horrible so I can't make any money." Groupon was started by Andrew Mason in the middle of the 2008 recession as a way small businesses could get broader exposure and offer discounts to get customers in the door. Today the company is worth over $700 million. Travis Kalanick and Garrett Camp thought up Uber in 2009 (also during the recession) when they were stuck and couldn't find a taxi on a cold night. It has expanded its services to include things like food delivery and is now worth about $47 Billion. They all knew that circumstances—a rotten economy—didn't have to determine their success.

Physical issues: Take something like a severe disability. I'm guessing that most of us would assume that a severe disability meant you would have to live a small and confined life. But I can show you hundreds of examples of people who didn't. Nicholas Vujicic was born with no arms and no legs. Talk about a huge difficult circumstance! His mother was so upset, she refused to even hold him and walked out of the hospital! Today? He's graduated from college, has a successful career as an author and public speaker, is married with 4 children, and types 43 words per minute with his toes! Daryl Mitchell was a very successful actor who had a horrendous motorcycle accident in 2001 that left him paralyzed from the waist down. I think a lot of actors would have given up at that point. But he went on to act in several movies and a bunch of TV shows like NCIS. He now advocates for younger actors with disabilities.

Helen Keller was born blind and deaf. She went on to earn a bachelor's degree, wrote 12 books, and received the Presidential Medal of honor for her work with the blind. When she was just 13, Bethany Hamilton was attacked by a shark and lost her left arm. Two years later, she won a national title and is now a professional surfer. Marlee Matlin lost her hearing when she was little, but she became an actor and won the Oscar's Award for Best Actress in a Leading Role by age 21.

So, does the circumstance of physical problems *really* determine your life? I don't think these people were naturally exceptional. But they did develop exceptional mindsets! And you can too. Circumstances have an *impact* on our lives for sure, but they don't *determine* our lives. What determines our lives is the *story* we decide to tell and what we *do* with them.

Guarding the Portal
of Your Mind

You are the sum total of everything you've ever seen, heard, eaten, smelled, been told, forgot—it's all there. Everything influences each of us, and because of that I try to make sure that my experiences are positive.
— *Maya Angelou*

Imagine that you are making yourself a great big healthy salad with beautiful orange carrots, garden fresh tomatoes, crispy lettuce, and crunchy celery. You might throw in some bright red bell peppers, some creamy avocado, some spicy red onion, and a few garbanzo beans—all the fixings of your perfect salad! (Okay, if you hate vegetables, make yourself a sandwich!) Then you throw all of these awesome, colorful veggies in a gorgeous bowl, and toss them together. It's perfect!

Then you pour battery acid over it.

So, a) I've never actually done this, and I would NOT recommend it and b) I know you would never do this *intentionally*.

But are you *unintentionally* doing it to your mindset? Are you trying to think positive thoughts and rewrite your moldy old negative stories but pouring battery acid all over your mindset through your daily habits? If you haven't spent a lot of time being aware of your mindset before, you've probably gotten into habits that the majority of people have. These habits might look "normal" but I'm telling you that they will *eat away* at all your efforts to improve your mindset like that battery acid! You need to create an environment that is positive and supports what you really want in life, whether it's financial success, a healthier body, or more loving relationships. You need to "stand guard at the portal" of your mind. You need to make sure that what goes into your mind uplifts you and makes you feel more capable and stronger. That means you need to cut out the junk you've been feeding it!

You have to ditch some toxic habits to give your mindset a healthy environment. I put these toxic habits into 3 categories: mental junk food, hanging out with negative people, and being sloppy with your words.

Mental Junk Food

"Humans have a knack for choosing precisely the things that are worst for them."
—*J. K. Rowling*

Too many people pay little or *no* attention at all to what they let into their brains! Not all of our limiting beliefs or negative thoughts and assumptions come from our own personal experiences or our past. A lot of it comes from the "mental junk food" we surround ourselves with. We all know that junk food isn't good for us, right? As yummy as those nachos taste, we know we shouldn't eat them too much or too often—unless we're trying to grow into a bigger size of jeans! Junk food can feel like comfort food at the time, but it actually can make us feel pretty crummy afterwards, doesn't it? Have you ever eaten a whole tub of your favorite ice cream in one sitting? Fun at the time but, trust me, your body will let you know really soon afterwards that it was a rotten idea!

Most of us are pretty clear that "garbage in means garbage out" when it comes to eating and our bodies. If we want to be healthy, we need to eat healthy food. It's exactly the same with your mindset. If you want a really healthy mindset, one that helps you get what you truly want out of life, you need to feed it really *healthy* mind food.

But most people feed their minds—the most precious resource they have—with any old thing that comes along. They watch the doom and gloom of the news every day. They watch the Weather Channel where it seems like there's some huge natural disaster every other day. They pay attention and listen when their co-workers complain and whine. They scroll through all the arguing and bickering on Facebook for hours. They'll read books and articles that tell us the world is a mess.

The thing is, it's like overeating junk food. At the time, it feels good, almost addictive. For some crazy reason, it feels satisfying to complain with your neighbor, listen to people talking about how horrible the economy is or how rotten politicians are, or read about the latest celebrity scandal on Facebook, right? But when you let yourself do those things, you're destroying the most powerful tool in your toolbox: your healthy mindset. It's like you have this amazing thoroughbred horse that could win the Kentucky Derby—but you're feeding it Captain Crunch and malt liquor. You're turning your champion horse into a broken-down old nag just by what you're feeding it. And that's what most people do with their mindsets.

The National Science published an article in 2005 about the research into the number of thoughts people have every day. They said that we have anywhere from 12,000 to 60,000 thoughts per day. Not all of them are great big, brilliant thoughts. A lot are like "Where did I put my keys?" or "What do I want for lunch today?" Still, 60,000 seems like a lot of thoughts. But what was more interesting is that *85% of those thoughts were negative* and 95% were thoughts that we've thought over and over a thousand times!

Negativity Sells

> *"You cannot have a positive life and a negative mind."*
> —Joyce Meyer

Why so much negativity? Unless you live in a cave, you're *surrounded* by negativity. And the reason that you see so much negativity is because market research shows that *negative news gets more attention than positive news*. It's like all those people who can't help but rubberneck at a bad car crash. If there was a story about 23 babies getting saved from a burning building, that might get attention for a day or an hour. But if the story was that 23 babies *died* in a burning building, people would be talking about it for years.

There's so much negativity because negativity works. The Bad Wolf amygdala is absolutely addicted to it! Bad news helps the Bad Wolf build its case that the world is a horrible scary place, and you should hide out in your comfort zone to stay safe. If we aren't careful, we get bombarded with negativity from our news feeds, in our inboxes, the news we watch or read. Our Bad Wolf gets stronger. Our thoughts and emotions react to all that negativity, and they determine the action we're willing to take.

Think about it. If you watch the news regularly, how do you feel afterwards? Do you feel upbeat, positive, excited about life? Or do you feel angry, sad, depressed about the future, and maybe anxious or scared? Will any of those feelings help you make great decisions or motivate you to go for your dreams? I don't think so.

Personally, I haven't watched the news for about 17 years. The only time I watch any news is when I'm at my parents' house, because they're obsessed with it and they watch it all the time. And I had a boyfriend a long time ago who loved the news. I ended up breaking up with him because he was so negative and unhappy—probably because he watched the darn news so much! I urge you to limit your news consumption. Look, do we really need to be tuned in 24/7? Most of what we hear on the news or on Google isn't accurate anyway. The media specializes in the negative and dramatic. They know we're drawn to a bloody car accident or a raging fire.

When I talk about avoiding the junk food that the news focuses on, I don't mean that you should deny what's going on in the world. We need to stay informed to a certain extent. But we don't need to know every little detail about problems we have no control over and can do nothing about. We don't need to be constantly feeding ourselves with news that makes us feel angry, helpless, victimized, or fearful.

If you absolutely must know what's going on, find a source of news that is less sensational. Check out what's happening maybe once a day—or once a week! When you watch or listen to the news, ask yourself, "Is this something I really need to know? Is this something I can do something about? Is this something that is helpful to me and my family?" Even ask yourself, "Is this even true (or just what someone wants me to think or believe)?" If it doesn't benefit you, turn it off! Better yet, if you want some positive news, tune into The Good News Network or Positive News. Fill your brain with positive and hopeful news. Actually, when you start to look for it, you can find a lot: people being generous and doing good for others, people overcoming big odds to become successful, people inventing awesome things to solve world problems. It's there if you hunt for it. (The Good Wolf will thank you!)

One way I see students get affected negatively by the news is when they follow economic forecasts. If everyone is saying the economy is "bad," they're convinced they won't be able to succeed. That is absolutely not true! I always tell my students that the market is in between your ears. It's what you *tell* yourself it is! The people and businesses that got innovative and responded to hard times didn't fall apart when the economy tanked. They actually prospered:

During the Depression in the 1930s, people couldn't afford mayonnaise anymore because its ingredients were so expensive. So, Kraft came up with Miracle Whip that had cheaper ingredients but could be used as a spread like mayonnaise. Because it was much cheaper, people were still able to buy it.

Also in the 1930s, Michael Cullen had the idea for the first modern "supermarket," a store that had tons of goods at discounted prices and was totally self-service. His boss at Kroger didn't believe that this new concept would ever work, so Cullen took off and started his own store, King Cullen. By 1932 he had a chain of 8 stores. He succeeded because he paid attention to the times and offered Depression-era prices.

Kellogg's, the famous cereal maker, also prospered during the Depression by doing some things that seemed counterintuitive. First, they renovated their workforce, reducing hours by giving them the *same pay for a 6-hour day* then *hiring more people* for other jobs (that 6-hour day got to 8-hour productivity levels within 2 years). They also started advertising heavily where other companies were backing off. They ended up with a totally loyal, committed workforce—and Rice Krispies ended up on just about every breakfast table in America!

These people knew what was going on, but they didn't buy into the doom and gloom predictions that the news was making. They paid attention and said, "Okay, how can I get creative with what's going on?" But to do that, you need to start with a confident mindset. You need to start by believing, "If it can be done, I can do it." I have my own personal story about this.

Throughout my real estate career, I always researched market trends. I tried to be proactive and figure out where the real estate market was headed in the future. In the years 2005-2007, we had a fantastic seller's market. Sounds great but I realized that home prices were increasing way too fast! Homes that were the same model on the very same street would jump from $400,000 to $460,00 or even $500,000 in just one day! My parents bought a house for $503,000. Just two years and 1 day later, they sold it for $1,170,000! More than double! That's crazy and it was a crazy time. People were refinancing their mortgages all over the place and taking out huge loans that they could barely afford. Common sense told me that it couldn't last, and the bubble was bound to burst.

The first thing that occurred to me is that people would soon start losing their homes. I knew we were going to have a problem. I started contacting banks, traveling the country, and going to bankers' association conferences. By the time the real estate market completely crashed in 2008, I had already started going to banking foreclosure conferences and establishing relationships with banks and asset managers.

I also got creative and put some skin in the game. I sent packages to asset managers all over the country. I put these packages in a folder with a pair of socks on it and some pop rocks on the front that said, "Let me pop your socks off." My resume was inside with what I could offer, a list of my contractors and proof that I knew how to do a Broker Price Opinion (which was like a little mini appraisal), all things that were important to a bank. I had to learn the business, get creative, be resourceful and be willing to put the work in *before* there was any guarantee of a payoff in it. But I believed and knew if I did all of that, something would come of it. And it did.

By being proactive, thinking ahead, educating myself about foreclosures, and doing my research, I landed the accounts of several banks and asset management companies to help them sell the homes they foreclosed on. It was sad and depressing and I'd never want to do that kind of business again. But at the time, it was survival. Many agents lost their homes, careers, and disappeared—until the market got easy again several years later.

By the time the market totally crashed, I was already working with thirteen different banks selling their foreclosures. By then, it was almost too late for anyone else to get in, make the connections they needed, and gain the expertise it takes to sell foreclosures. From 2008 to 2014, my focus was foreclosures and short sales.

None of this happened by accident. I paid attention to industry news, but I didn't let it freak me out. I took the facts, not the negative spin everyone was giving it, and positioned myself to respond to what was happening while everyone else was ignoring the situation or sitting around worrying about it.

> I took the facts, not the negative spin everyone was giving it, and positioned myself to respond to what was happening while everyone else was ignoring the situation or sitting around worrying about it.

And it all had to do with my mindset. I did *not* believe that I was helpless in the face of a "bad" market. I had enough confidence in myself that I could figure out a way to keep my business thriving despite what was going on. Was I a little worried at first? Sure! But I didn't keep listening to the doom and gloom that would have added to that worry. I took action instead.

Wasting Time on Worry

Worry is like a rocking chair: it gives you something to do but never gets you anywhere. —Erma Bombeck

For the most part, mental junk food usually adds to our worry and anxiety levels. Worry and anxiety is all about *imagining* something bad is going to happen in the future. The thing you're worrying about hasn't happened yet and may not ever happen, right? But you imagine the worst. And if you've ever told yourself that you don't have a great imagination, don't kid yourself. Just think about your teenager or your spouse being 3 hours late getting home one night. You come up with all kinds of stories about what could have happened, right? And I'll bet you that not many of them sound like, "Oh, they're probably fine and just forgot to look at the clock." Your body starts to feel panicked and the more time that passes, the worse and worse your stories become. That's a terrible waste of your creative imagination!

A study out of Cornell University found that 85% of what we worry about *never happens*. Of the worries that actually *did* happen, 79% of the subjects said that either it turned out they could handle what they'd worried about much better than they'd thought or that the things they worried about had taught them some kind of valuable lesson.

Obviously, we're wasting a heck of a lot of valuable brain power and undermining our mindset at the same time! The news is full of all kinds of horrible stories that get you thinking, "What if that happened to me?" They make it sound like bad guys or horrible accidents or dangerous weather are all around you! The news has got you sucked into bad things that haven't happened to you. Yet your worried thoughts are scaring you with the idea that it *might*.

Worry is a waste of time. It makes you miserable and nervous. It doesn't help you to be creative or proactive, it just drives you crazy. The truth is, even if some of our fears *do* happen, if we keep a strong and healthy mindset, we'll be *much* more capable of taking positive action to respond to it. Don't let the negativity of the news media rob you of that. Just turn it off!

Eliminate Worry and Anxiety

If you do find yourself worrying, whether about something in the news or something else, don't let it sabotage your mindset. Stay aware of how you're feeling and remember your Stop, Snap and Switch, only this time it will be Stop, Snap and Prepare. In this case, the switch might be, "Okay, so if this thing *does* happen, what can I do about it?" You can't stop something like a hurricane or a wildfire, but even for things like that you can almost always get prepared.

Another way to snap out of anxiety is by using the Stop, Snap, and Remember. It starts the same. When you notice the negative worry, stop and snap your wristband. Then as you switch your band to the other wrist you bring up a memory of a time when you overcame a difficulty. Think about this time and what helped you through it. Were you creative? Calm? Did you take action? By reminding yourself of all the times you've overcome difficulties, you're strengthening that resiliency pathway. As you really get into feeling how great it felt to face and overcome a difficulty, you suddenly feel much more capable of facing whatever you're worried about. You've loosened up the worry so you can start finding positive solutions.

If you find that you're *constantly* worrying a lot about all kinds of things, take charge of your mindset by using this practice.

1. Set up a specific worry time, say, 15 minutes in the late afternoon.

2. Write down anything you notice that you're worried about during the day but save it for your "worry appointment."

3. When you get to your worry appointment, check your list and ask, "How valid or true is that worry? How likely is it to happen?" Cross off the ones that seem unlikely or that don't really make sense.

4. Look at the rest of your list and mark the ones that are *not* in your control and the ones that are in your control.

5. Think about the worst that could happen if these worries came true.

6. Do your Stop, Snap, and Remember exercise and think about times you've overcome difficulties. Allow yourself to remember the feeling of being strong and capable.

7. Next, Stop, Snap and Prepare. Brainstorm ideas for handling the worst that could happen for the things that *are* in your control.

8. Accept the things that are *not* in your control and figure out how you could prepare for them.

The Drain of Social Media

Another huge source of negative input for a lot of people is social media. Social media has a lot of helpful information and great inspiration. It can have posts that make you laugh out loud which is always a good thing, and you can find out what's up with friends you don't see all that often. Unfortunately, it's also become a place where a lot of people vent anger and frustration, spread misinformation (often without knowing it), and complain about anything and everything! If you still want to spend time on social media (which, face it, can be a huge waste of time unless you're using it to promote your business), do yourself a big favor and clear all the Whiney Wandas and Angry Andys off your feeds! You don't have to unfriend them. You can just opt to *not* see their posts.

One of my best friends, Raquel, has a son, Triston Otis, who told me about a thing called "toxic positivity" and since then, I've noticed it a lot on social media. Toxic positivity is when someone writes a post like, "Just having a bad day, not feeling good about myself today." And then the whole news feed gets flooded with people telling them how great they are or trying to lift them up. Now I really believe that supporting people is good. But a lot of times, people are pumping people up who don't need to be pumped up. These people fish for a flood of support from the outside day after day. They need to just get out of their funk and make stuff happen. Rather than waiting for the world to make them feel good, they need to look within to feel better and to grow. Some people just love to play the victim in life and their "supporters" are not helping them get stronger but enabling them to stay whiney and dependent.

People also use social media to feel bad about themselves, seeing all the great things people post about their awesome romance or their fancy trips or brand new cars. They compare these posts to their own life and feel like they're failing somehow. But the truth of the matter is that a lot of people just post all the *good* stuff so it appears that they have the perfect life. We see their "perfect life" and feel ours isn't as good—only to find out that a week later they're in divorce court or filing for bankruptcy—or both! Don't do that to yourself. Comparison is never a good idea but especially when you're comparing yourself to something that is just a fairytale version of someone's life. As Theodore Roosevelt said, "Comparison is the thief of joy."

Instead of getting caught up in all the negative garbage, use the internet to Google the good! You've got free access to all kinds of inspiration online, from music to TedTalks to uplifting poetry. Rather than checking out the news or Facebook when your brain is feeling the munchies for outside input, try searching out something positive like "inspirational quotes" or "happy music." Give your brain something healthy and positive to munch on rather than more stuff to worry about or upset you.

It takes some effort to change that mental junk food habit. But if you're serious about a mindset that brings you success in life, you've got to replace the junk food with a constant diet of healthy food. I have literally hundreds of inspirational, uplifting audio books. I listen to them while I'm cooking, driving, and getting ready in the morning. If you don't have this kind of material on hand, get some. You can also check out apps that have positive messages like ThinkUp or training courses like SkillShare or Mastermind.com. Listen to them while you do chores or read them right before you turn out the light at night. Ask friends for recommendations about books or apps that have made a difference in their lives. Make sure you're reading and listening to material that makes you feel good about yourself and where you're going, that teaches you something and helps you grow. That's what the Good Wolf is hungry for!

And remove yourself from negative conversations as well. Do you really need to hear the latest workplace gossip? Do you really need to argue about politics with your sister-in-law again? Do you really need to listen to your co-worker bash her boss? Do any of those conversations make you feel happy, positive, and empowered? You're a free agent! You don't have to engage in these kinds of conversations. You can change the subject or, if that doesn't work, get the heck out of there.

Negative Nellies in Your Life

"We are the average of the five people we spend the most time with."
—*Jim Rohn*

Okay, I know that this has been a touchy subject for a lot of my students so it might be for you. It's about all the people you hang out with on a regular basis. In "guarding the portal of your mind," you need to be *especially* careful about the people you spend a lot of time with. They are the ones that will have the most influence on your mindset. They can either help you get stronger and more confident, or they can eat away at that strength and confidence and make you feel uncertain and hesitant to go for your dreams. How do you know which they are? Just notice how you feel after spending time with them. Do you feel great about yourself and ready to conquer the world? Are you smiling and upbeat? Or do you feel down and drained? Do you leave them feeling anxious and worried?

Some people are just plain negative. They find something wrong with *everything* and love to complain. No matter what is happening, it's not good enough for them. They may not criticize you to your face, but they criticize everybody else, so you've got to assume they have some pretty strong judgments about you too. These are the people who make sure that everyone knows their troubles and how awful those troubles are. If the people you see and interact with on a daily basis are doom and gloom Negative Nellies, it will be tough to keep your momentum moving forward.

Does this mean you need to ditch the friends you've had since kindergarten? Maybe, but that's up to you and it depends on how much negative influence they have on you. At the very least, you want to identify the people that are sucking the juice and enthusiasm out of you and spend less time around them. You also don't want to share your most cherished dreams and goals with that kind of person. They'll only try to pop holes in your balloon.

People are either energy givers or energy takers. Energy givers are like a fully charged battery that can literally light up a room or get something moving like crazy. Energy takers are like a dead battery. It does nothing and contributes nothing. There are people that you meet or hang out with who are energetic, positive, happy, supportive and enthusiastic. Those are the people you want to be around more because they inspire you, motivate you, and make you feel good. And then there are energy takers who are always down and out, always doom and gloom. Nothing ever goes right with them. They are complainers and always see the worst in things. And they give *you* the worst of themselves and *push their negative energy onto you.*

We want to be around positive energy givers and be energy givers ourselves. As an energy giver, you'll find people want to be around you more, and more positive things happen to your personal life and your business or career. One reason my coaching business has taken off so much is that I'm an energy giver. I pass my positive energy onto people, and they want more of it. So, ask yourself, are you an energy giver or taker? Work at being a giver everywhere you go and see what happens in your life.

Rather than the Negative Nellies or the energy drainers, you want to surround yourself with people who are positive and going after their own goals and dreams so you can be a cheering squad for each other. And if you don't have friends like this? You need to find some! Check out different organizations in your community like Rotary Clubs and Toastmasters groups. They often cater to people who are heading forward in life, not moaning about the past and what "can't" be done.

Dr. Sonja Lyubomirsky from UC Riverside published a review of 225 studies in the American Psychological Association. What all those studies showed is that "chronically happy" people generally achieve more success in all areas of life than people who are usually not happy. Her review said that this was because "... happy people frequently experience positive moods and these positive moods prompt them to be more likely to work actively toward new goals and build new resources. When people feel happy, they tend to feel confident, optimistic, and energetic and others find them likable and sociable. Happy people are thus able to benefit from these perceptions." Dr. Lyubomirsky also wrote that it wasn't their success that made them happy but their happiness that led to their success "... and happy individuals are more likely than their less happy peers to have fulfilling marriages and relationships, high incomes, superior work performance, community involvement, robust health and even a long life."

it wasn't their success that made them happy but their happiness that led to their success

In Dan Sullivan's book *The Gap and The Gain,* he talks about a study of 180 nuns. When they first became nuns in the 20s, they were asked to write autobiographical journals. Then 50+ years later, researchers looked at the nuns' journals and separated those who had written more positive things from those who were more negative. They found that the nuns who had written more joyful and positive things and about their positive emotions lived an average of 10 years longer than nuns who had written negative or neutral things. By age 85, 90% percent of the happy/positive nuns were still alive compared to only 34% percent of the unhappy or less happy nuns! If that doesn't motivate you to spend more time with happier people and get happier yourself, I don't know what will! You have the control to be happier. You have a choice!

What about the people in your life who aren't outright negative, but they don't believe in your dreams? Sometimes the people who love us the most are afraid we'll get hurt or fail. They care about us, so they want us to be safe. They've listened to their own Bad Wolf and think we should listen too.

I was 46 years old when I made the decision that I wanted to be a coach. I had been reading *Think and Grow Rich* and it talked about how we often have this constant nagging from the Universe telling us to do something. I knew for me it was coaching but my career in real estate was going so well, I just kept pushing it back.

But I was at a point in my life where I was ready. I just jumped on it. I had a meeting with my dad and mom (two of my most favorite people in the world) and my husband Steve (the love of my life and of course, another of my most favorite people in the world). So, I sat down to tell them about my plan to become a coach. And they were like, "Krista, we love you. But you really should think about this. Normal people don't leave at 46 years old to change careers when they're bringing home over a million dollars a year. No one is going to pay you to coach them. It's just not a good idea. We love you, we know you're amazing, but you should really rethink this."

These are the people that love me and support me the most, my dad, my mom and my husband, who want the best for me and truly are my biggest supporters. They were trying to help me and protect me. But literally if I had listened to them and their advice and not gone with my true gut instinct, the universe pulling me into the direction of coaching, I would not be where I'm at right now. And quite frankly, I would be miserable because I was at a point in my career where I was totally exhausted and tired. I didn't even realize just how exhausted and tired I was until I was coaching full time.

Had I not listened to my gut and my heart and the Universe pulling me, had I listened to the people who really love me and wanted to help me, I would not be nearly as happy as I am now. I was happy before but now I feel so fulfilled and like I'm making a real contribution. The more that I contribute to the world, the more I'm growing. And now, instead of making a million dollars in a year, I recently had a $4 million month this year. (That's not typical, but my goal is for it to be typical soon!) Of course, I have 50 employees that get paid out of that, but my take-home pay is definitely not shabby!

So, with people who are generally positive and supportive but protective of you, just be careful when you share with them what you really want. Listen to what they say but trust your gut and heart. Check and see whether their advice is feeding the Good Wolf or the Bad Wolf.

And make sure you take advice from people who have been where you want to go. You wouldn't go to your hair stylist for her advice on your car and you probably wouldn't ask your mechanic what to do with your hair. If you wanted advice on your tennis game, you'd go to a pro, not your neighbor who's never played the game or who just barely knows how to hold a racket. I love my family and they're all successful in their own way. But none of them have ever built multi-million dollar businesses. In getting advice about building a coaching business, I needed to talk to people who were already successful doing it at the level I wanted. (Dad, when you're reading this, don't hate me lol! I love you and think you're brilliant!)

Who Do You Want in Your Life?

Start by drawing a big circle on a piece of paper. Then draw a smaller one inside of it and an even smaller one inside of that one. In the smallest circle in the center, write the names of all of the people who are closest to you, the people you see on a daily basis or that you live with, the people that have the most influence over you. On the next bigger circle, write the names of people who are good friends or maybe family that you see often but not every day. On the outside circle, write names of people you consider friends or family but you're not especially close with.

Now, sit and think about the names in the circles. Which ones feed you good energy, support you, inspire you, make you feel good about who you are and what you're doing? Which ones drain energy from you, make you feel inadequate or down, who always try to pop your balloon?

Pay attention to which circle they're in. Which ones do you want to spend more time with? Which people should you spend *less* time with? Or, in the case of people you live with, how can you set it up so that your time together is more positive for both of you?

Your Words: Power or Poison

Most people tend to be pretty sloppy with their words. How often do you hear or say things like, "I'm such an idiot!" or "I'm sick and tired of this!" or "She's such a pain in the neck!"? Most people hardly even think about what they're saying because they assume the words don't matter. They know that they aren't really an idiot and that their neck doesn't really hurt every time they see that obnoxious co-worker. But the thing is that these *words do matter*, much more than you think.

I read an article[2] a while back that talked about a study where they found that Twitter was a great predictor of rates of coronary heart disease! Seriously, *Twitter*?!? Yep. Not only that but Twitter could predict rates of heart disease more *accurately* than other factors like obesity, smoking or low income. How did Twitter do it? *By the words people used.* They studied Tweets that came from different counties for a year. Then they compared the number of negative words used within each county to the number of deaths caused by heart disease. They found that when people tweeted a lot of negative words like "I'm exhausted" or "I'm so pissed off" or "Life sucks," people in that county had a much higher risk of heart disease than counties that tended to tweet a bunch of positive messages like "I'm so happy" or "It's going to be awesome!" Even when they looked at the other factors like obesity, smoking, lack of exercise, etc., the negative Tweets were still much better at predicting which counties had the highest rates of heart disease death. As one researcher put it: "The relationship between language and mortality is particularly surprising, since the people tweeting angry words and topics are in general not the ones dying of heart disease. But that means if many of your neighbors are angry, you are more

---

2   https://penntoday.upenn.edu/news/twitter-can-predict-rates-coronary-heart-disease-according-penn-research

likely to die of heart disease." Go to KristaMashore.com/SSSBook if you want to see the graphic showing this.

The words you use affect the people around you, but the words with the greatest impact are the words you use talking to yourself in your very own head! They will affect your emotions, your attitude, your willingness to try, your hormones, even what you notice around you. If you constantly say, "Life stinks" you'll tune in to all the stink bombs around you. If you constantly say, "This is so hard!" your body automatically responds by feeling tired and stressed. If you're always saying, "I have no money." Then you'll never have any money.

I remember feeling really tired after getting Covid and the tiredness lasted over a year. I was going to the gym with my girlfriend and we both kept saying, "Man, I'm so tired." One day I looked at her and I said "Shelley, we need to stop saying that we are so tired. The more we say it the more our brains will try to prove us right. We just have to stop." She agreed and it's amazing how quickly we noticed not feeling as tired anymore! Recently a friend of mine, Marcos, was in the gym saying how tired he was. I told him the story about the decision Shelley and I made, and I encouraged him to stop saying it and see how soon he will suddenly NOT feel so tired.

Try it for yourself. Take something simple that you do, like washing the dishes. Stand at the sink and say, "Ugh! It is so boring and difficult to get these dishes clean! I hate it!" Pay attention to how your body feels and how you feel emotionally. Now, try it again, only this time say, "Great! These will be done in no time! It's so easy and I'll have a clean kitchen when it's done!" Okay, so even if you don't quite believe yourself, how do you feel? More energetic and cheerful? What made the difference? The dishes didn't change. They didn't get dirtier or cleaner. The only thing that changed was what you told yourself about it.

Power Up Your Words

Make a list of things you normally complain about, even if it's just a small thing that you complain just a tiny bit about. Next, list what you say to yourself when you complain about it. It might be something like, "This is so boring" or "This is so hard" or "Why am I always the one stuck doing this?" Now do your Stop, Snap and Switch. When you switch, try on the opposite. In fact, sometimes it's fun to be outlandish with it. "This is so boring" can turn into "Oh, my gosh! This is so fascinating!" "This is so hard" can become "This is a piece of cake!" "Why am I always stuck with this" can become "Woo hoo! I won the prize! I get to be the one to do this again!" Your brain won't actually believe it, but it will probably make you laugh and lighten the mood.

Negative Self-Talk

As a kid, when someone teased me, I used that old saying of "Sticks and stones can break my bones, but words can never hurt me!" But the truth is, they did hurt me! They made me take on limiting beliefs like that I was stupid, ugly, that I didn't fit in, and all kinds of negative things about myself. I carried around a lot of the hurtful words from other kids, my early teachers and other people for decades. A broken bone would have definitely healed faster than those painful words did!

Most of us have had the experience of words that hurt us, like when I was called Miss Piggy. My brother is amazing, but he was just a kid and it wasn't meant to hurt me. But even unintentional words can hurt. And now research[3] has shown that negative words—spoken, heard, and maybe especially *thought* by a subject—cause reactions in the brain that release hormones related to stress and anxiety. These researchers concluded that "negative self-talk plays a role in the generation or maintenance of anxiety in normal children." In the book, *Words Can Change Your Brain,* the authors, Dr. Andrew Newberg, a neuroscientist and Mark Robert Waldman, an expert in communications, wrote, "Any form of negative rumination—for example, worrying about your financial future or health—will stimulate the release of destructive neurochemicals." They also looked at the impact of positive thoughts and words and noted that they stimulated the frontal lobe of the brain, the Good Wolf.

There's a ton of research now about how positive and negative self-talk affect performance, whether it's in sports or taking academic tests. I haven't run across *any* study that says that the words we use don't matter and don't affect how we feel and how we perform. So, this isn't just some happy-hippie idea. Your words are literally shaping your

---

3   https://pubmed.ncbi.nlm.nih.gov/9560177/

life. If you keep saying you don't have the time, you'll never have the time. If you keep saying you're broke and have no money, you'll never have the money. If you keep saying that you're exhausted, you'll stay tired. Have you ever said something to yourself about yourself that you would *never, ever* say to a loved one or dear friend? You wouldn't say it to them because you *know* it would be hurtful. So why would you say it to yourself? We have to pay attention to what we say because our thoughts become things. Words *do* matter.

The thing is, you cannot keep feeding yourself on a diet of negative words and limiting beliefs if you want to have the life you desire. You have to notice them and delete them every time they pop into your mind. How? Stop, Snap and Switch! Whenever you find yourself saying something like, "I'll never be able to do that," Stop, snap and switch your wristband and come up with another phrase like "I may not know how to do it now, but I know I can figure it out!"

Sometimes the words we use don't seem all that negative at the time. The most common one for most people is when people ask you how you are. What's the knee-jerk response? "Fine" or maybe "Good." Not super-negative but not super-positive either. What if you tried something different? A friend has a client who says, "I'm living the dream!" whenever she asks him how he's doing. It makes her laugh and feel good every time and I'm sure he feels better than "fine" after saying it, even if he didn't feel that great before. So, what could you say? "I'm doing awesome!" Or how about, "I'm having a great day!" It might feel weird at first but give it a shot and see how it changes your mood.

I read an article by a guy named James Clear. He's written a book called *Atomic Mind*. And he wrote that eliminating one word that we use all the time can make a huge difference to how we approach our daily lives. He says to just switch out "have to" for "get to." It seems too simple, right? But then I tried it for myself and found that it made a huge difference.

See, when you say you *have to* do something, it's as if you're being forced to do something. It's like a burden and it drains your energy. You might even feel a little grumpy about it. But when you say that you *get to* do the same thing, it's like a privilege or an adventure! Woo hoo! You get all excited and feel lucky that you *get to* do whatever it is!

Try it for yourself for a few days. Practice with your small *have to's* first. For example, start with "I *have to* take out the trash" and switch it to "I *get to* take out the trash" or "I *have to* go work out" and switch to "I *get to* go work out." As you make the switch, really notice the difference in how you feel. (Actually, the first times I tried it, I felt kinda goofy but it was better than feeling like what I was doing was a big burden!) Next, try it out on bigger issues like "I *get* to fire that vendor who isn't performing" or "I *get to* pay my taxes." (I mean think about it. In most cases, you *get* to pay taxes because you're making a lot of money!) Once you've experienced the difference, work on making *get to* a habit.

Seriously, just changing that one little phrase, from "*have to*" to "*get to*", sets off a whole different response in your body and emotions. *That's* the power of words. Your brain is paying attention. The Good Wolf and Bad Wolf are both waiting to see who's going to get fed.

You may not be aware of all the negative things that you say to yourself or out loud. Take one day to really focus on it. Listen to yourself, especially words and phrases you use over and over. Even if something you're telling yourself is not horribly negative, is there something else you could say that would be more positive and supportive? That would make you feel stronger and more upbeat? Use your Stop, Snap and Switch whenever it pops up again.

The Power of Your Body on Your Mind

I've talked a lot about how changing your thoughts and your emotions affects your physical nervous system. Well, the opposite is true as well. Our physical health and the way we use our bodies can have a huge impact on our mindset, our thoughts, our emotions, and even our beliefs. The idea about the mind/body connection has been in the mainstream for decades. Most people think of it in the direction of "mind over matter." But that connection runs both ways.

Yet, some of us treat our bodies like they're just vehicles for carrying our brains around. We spend much more time in our heads than being present in our bodies. We get so wrapped up in life that often we pay no attention to our bodies at all. We take them for granted until they break down—and *that's* when we realize how important our bodies are to the quality of our lives and our ability to reach our goals.

That's also when it becomes clear how much our physiology affects our mindset. Think back to a time when you were sick or injured. How easy was it to feel upbeat and cheerful? How easy was it to feel powerful, energetic, and purposeful? If you're like most of us, being sick or injured makes you feel grumpy, lethargic, and unenthusiastic about most anything except hiding under the covers! So, one of the first things you want to do to maintain a positive mindset is to stay (or get!) healthy. That includes all the basics: eating well, exercising, and getting enough rest. If you pay attention, you can notice how much sharper and more positive you feel when you do these things and research has proven why.

For example, our brains use up more than 20% of the calories we consume. Research has found that processes that lead to Alzheimer's and other forms of dementia begin years before anyone notices the symptoms. Studies found that the unhealthy foods we eat are the culprits because they create chronic inflammation in brain cells and blood vessels as our bodies try to break those foods down.

Exercise increases the blood circulation in the brain so that the brain gets all the nutrients it needs to carry out the millions of functions it has to manage on a daily basis. Exercise not only reduces anxiety, stress and depression, it also improves your brain's ability to think, learn, and problem-solve as well as improving memory. According to the *Journal of Clinical Psychiatry*, "Exercise improves mental health by reducing anxiety, depression, and negative mood and by improving self-esteem and cognitive function."

When it comes to getting enough sleep, the research is just as strong. For example, a study of school children showed that even one less hour of sleep resulted in more moodiness, depression and poorer grades as well as poorer reaction time, recall, and responsiveness compared to children who got an hour of sleep more. Researchers have discovered that sleep removes toxins in your brain that build up while you are awake. When you don't get enough sleep, you can't form new neuropathways, and it's harder to concentrate and respond quickly.

Shift Your Body to Shift Your Mindset

Your overall physical health is important to your mindset. And there are also techniques you can use your body to snap out of negative thoughts or emotions almost instantly. The way you stand, sit, walk and move has a huge impact on your mindset. There's plenty of research on this but it's pretty easy to prove it to yourself.

Try this: Sit in your chair all slumped over like you're bummed out and exhausted. After a moment or two, notice how you feel. How would that kind of feeling affect your thinking, your emotions, and energy level? Now stand up and put yourself in a Wonder Woman or Superman pose with your head up, chest out, shoulders back, hands on your hips and feet wide apart. Now how do you feel? Spend a few moments in that pose and notice how much more powerful, capable, confident and positive you feel.

Next, try this small posture shift that I learned from Tony Robbins: Lift your breastbone just a quarter of an inch. You don't have to stick out your chest to any extreme. Just a subtle lift. Notice a difference? You may not always be able to strike the Superhero pose but even in the middle of the grocery store, you can do this little rib cage lift to feel better.

How about walking? Do you ever wake up and stumble out of bed then shuffle to the bathroom in a fog? Try this instead: Sit up on the side of the bed. Take a deep breath. Say out loud, "Today is going to be a great day!" and immediately think of one thing you are grateful for. Stand up strongly and firmly on both feet then march to the bathroom with energy. A much better way to start your day! You're signaling your mind and body that you're alive, awake, alert, and enthusiastic!

Now try just walking around your home or office as you normally do. Notice your normal pace of walking and how you feel. Next, stride around your home or office as if you're king or queen of your castle. Walk as if you're a very significant, impressive person with important things to do! Walk *as if* you feel powerful and what happens? You begin to feel powerful.

The next time you notice that you aren't feeling as capable and powerful as you'd like to feel, just try a Stop, Snap, and March or a Stop,

Snap, and Superhero. It's also great to use these physical tools right before you have to go into a big meeting or before a conversation that might be difficult.

Are you feeling a positive difference when you use these techniques? If so, help me help others experience that same difference by leaving a review of my book on Amazon. Thank you!

Your Breathing

Another physical way to shift a negative mindset is to breathe. I know that sounds crazy because, of course, you're breathing or you wouldn't be alive to read this! But even though you're breathing, you may not be breathing *properly*.

You know how when you feel panicked or really angry, and someone says, "Just take a deep breath"? Well, it actually works. Deep breathing signals your parasympathetic nervous system to slow your heart rate down and release hormones that make you feel calm. That's why you'll see performers and athletes who are about to do their thing take a few deep breaths first. A lot of us do it unconsciously. We'll take a deep breath before a difficult meeting or a tricky phone call. We'll take a deep breath before trying to do something that's challenging for us.

I use deep breathing when I wake up at night to stop my mind racing and help me fall back asleep. Sometimes in the middle of the night, I wake up feeling a bit of anxiety. Deep breathing releases any anxiety and calms my thoughts. Just about all forms of meditation use deep breathing to relax the body and calm the mind. They often call it "belly breathing."

Belly breathing is the kind of breathing a baby does. If you watch a little kid sleeping, you can see that their tummy rises when they inhale and drops when they exhale. They're fully relaxed. As adults, many of us aren't so relaxed when we breathe. Our breathing is shallow, not deep. Instead of the tummy inflating, our chests rise and fall as we breathe. That's a clear sign that you're not breathing deeply.

Some forms of meditation just suggest breathing into your belly and paying attention to your breath. Others are more specific and recommend 4-7-8 breathing which is: Breathe in for four seconds, hold your breath for seven seconds, then exhale for eight seconds and repeat. Because you're counting the seconds, you naturally stay focused on your breath.

I read once about the type of breathing Navy SEALS are trained to do. Navy SEALS are in horribly stressful situations all the time. To survive in those situations, they need to remain calm and focused, right? So, they learn something called Box Breathing to help them stay calm and centered so they can deal with whatever they're facing. It goes like this:

Inhale for four seconds. Then hold the air in your lungs for four seconds. Next, exhale for four seconds. Then pause for another four seconds before inhaling again. You do this five times or more until you feel calm again. It's so simple.

You can find a bunch of breathing techniques online. All of them are effective but you'll probably find one you like better than others. It might take a while to get the hang of deep breathing. Just find a breathing pattern that works for you and make a point to practice it each night when you lie down to go to sleep. The more you do it, the more natural it will become.

Then, when you realize you need more calm or focus during the day, you can Stop, Snap, and Breathe!

Laughter and Smiling

When was the last time you really laughed? Most little kids, even babies, laugh a lot. It's said that the average 4-year-old laughs 300 times a day. But the average 40-year-old only laughs *four* times a day. Little kids will laugh at just about anything. They love to be silly, and they play with everything, even their food. But as we become big, serious, important adults, our sense of play and ability to laugh at everything gets drummed out of us.

Scientific research has shown that laughter, especially when you're laughing with other people, relaxes the body, increases blood flow, releases endorphins, and even burns calories! It brings people closer together and eases anxiety. It can not only boost your immune system, but it is an instant stress reliever and helps you stay grounded, focused and alert. It also helps you release negative emotions. When you really laugh, it's pretty much impossible to hang on to anger, depression, or frustration, so it's a perfect tool to help you switch out of a stinky mindset. Putting a big smile on your face has the same effect.

The trick is to find something to laugh about when you're stuck feeling negative, right? But you don't need some outside trigger to get yourself to laugh. There's a type of yoga called Laughter Yoga that encourages you to just start laughing at nothing, even if it feels a little weird. You can start with a fake Santa Claus laugh. Keep at it for a few moments and it seems so silly that it becomes a real laugh. You can also just put a great big old grin on your face. Smiling and laughter lets your nervous system know that all is well, and your thoughts and emotions respond by being more positive.

So next time you notice that you're feeling generally gloomy or irritable, just Stop, Snap, and Laugh or Grin!

The Prison: Your Comfort Zone

Security is mostly a superstition. It does not exist in nature, nor do the children of men as a whole experience it. Avoiding danger is no safer in the long run than outright exposure. Life is either a daring adventure, or nothing.
—Helen Keller

We all know what a comfort zone is, right? It's the place that we feel perfectly at home, totally on top of everything, relaxed and snug as a bug in a rug. We know who we are and what we're doing. It's easy and familiar. We feel in control and we feel confident that we know what we're doing. What could possibly be wrong with that? Really just one thing: It's keeping you from having what you really want out of life!

You probably have one of those thermostats at home where you can pre-set the temperature to a comfy range, your comfort zone. For instance, you might have it set at 70-72 degrees. When it gets colder than that, your heater comes on to bring it back to your comfort zone. When it gets too hot for your comfort, the AC kicks in to cool it down. It's automatic and you don't even have to think about it. And you *never* have to be too uncomfortable. Great, huh?

But not so great when we're talking about the comfort zones that rule our lives and limit us, keeping what we think we can do or be or have within a narrow, little range based on making sure we're always "comfortable."

In life, our comfort zones are determined by the fears of the Bad Wolf and our limiting beliefs. It can be conscious but a lot of it is unconscious. The comfort "settings" are automatic, and the neuropathways of these settings are pretty strong. You know you're out of your comfort zone when you feel uneasy, like you're not totally in control, maybe like you don't know what the heck you're doing. You can feel a little nervous or completely terrified. Your heart might be beating out of your chest, and it can feel hard to breathe. You're doing something that is not comfy, and *the Bad Wolf is not happy about it*!

We've got comfort zones in all kinds of areas: You've got a comfort zone for how much money you deserve to make, the kind of partner that would want you and who you want to be with, how far you can go in your career or in building your business, what you are capable of, etc. etc. Unless you've had a lot of experience in breaking free from your comfort zone, whenever you even start to reach a tiny step beyond it, you probably panic and then retreat to where it feels safe again.

By the way, remember how a thermostat keeps it comfy in *both* directions? When it's too cold, it turns up the heat. When it's too hot, it flips on the A/C. The comfort zones in your life are the same. When you fall *below* what the Bad Wolf has decided you're supposed to be or have, you get uncomfortable as well. For example, if you're stuck in a job that the Bad Wolf thinks is beneath you, you feel unhappy and restless and dissatisfied. The Bad Wolf ratchets up your feeling of discontent until you finally get off your rear and do something about it! That's not such a bad thing, right? However, if you reach for a job that the Bad Wolf thinks is *too good* for you, it'll make sure you feel so nervous that you blow the interview or so afraid that you never even apply for it!

Like the thermostat, your comfort zone works *automatically* without us even thinking about it. You start making more money than you think you deserve and, somehow, you'll unconsciously sabotage yourself until you're back to the kind of income you're comfortable with. Or you start making *less* money than you're comfortable with and your anxiety kicks in and pushes you to make more. Or maybe you start getting into better physical shape than the Bad Wolf has decided you should for whatever reason. Suddenly, you've got an injury or you "don't have time" to work out anymore. On the flip side, you might gain more weight than your comfort zone settings allow so you feel totally miserable and dissatisfied until you lose it.

The problem is that, if you hang around the *lower edges* of your comfort zone long enough—like being satisfied with being tight for money but not broke, or being little pudgy but not obese—you start to stretch that lower bar. Gaining a couple of pounds might still be in your comfort range. Then you gain a few more and it's not great but still okay. A few more pounds and you start to be uncomfortable but still not unhappy enough to do something about it—except maybe buy bigger jeans! With every extra pound that you let sneak in, over time you stretch that lower bar of your comfort zone by thinking, "It's not so bad. It could be worse."

Another example: if your partner isn't great but not *too* bad, you might be a little unhappy, but you can get comfortable with being a little unhappy. Then when they start doing something that hurts a little more, you can get used to being a *little more* unhappy. Your thermostat keeps setting the bar lower and lower until one day, you realize you just can't take it any longer! You can't stretch that lower edge any further. That's the point when people blow up in divorce or stomp out and quit the job they've had for twenty years or decide once and for all that they will not be in debt anymore and rip up all their credit cards and scream, "I've had it!"

So, does that mean you should hang out in the *upper* edges of your comfort zone? No! You don't want to stay in your comfort zone at all! You want to think of that upper bar as no longer acceptable and push through it! As Cher says, *"Until you're ready to look foolish, you'll never have the possibility of being great."*

> As Cher says, "Until you're ready to look foolish, you'll never have the possibility of being great."

As kids, we knew that the comfort zone is *not* the place we want to live forever. We knew we didn't want mom to tie our shoes for the rest of our lives or have training wheels on our bikes forever. We knew we'd never figure out how to bounce a basketball or play the piano if we didn't try it and probably look kinda dumb at first. As adults, we forget that. We bounce up against our comfort zone and use that as a sign that we're supposed to back off.

Let me be really clear with you: The comfort zone is not and has never been your friend. In fact, I always tell my students, if you're feeling overwhelmed and panicked, it's time to celebrate. Woo hoo! It means you're stretching beyond what you've known before and who you've been before. It's your opportunity to grow, learn and strive to be even more! The comfort zone is *not* your friend. It's a prison. So, don't be so eager to stay all huddled up, nice and cozy in it. The comfort zone was never intended as your final destination.

Think of Mohini, that tiger. She had a whole big, beautiful landscape to run in. It was right there being offered to her! But her comfort zone settings told her she could only have that tiny patch by the wall. What good stuff is waiting for you right outside your comfort zone? Because I'm telling you, there's a lot.

I talked about change earlier and your comfort zone is directly tied to the way you feel about change. Anything outside of your comfort zone will be a change for you, right? A lot of people (all comfy, cozy in their comfort zones) think change is a nasty word and they try to avoid it at all costs (which is actually impossible in life! Change is going to happen to you in the end, no matter how you feel about it!). Yet the way you decide to handle change determines whether you succeed or fail in life.

Let me just repeat that: The way you decide to handle change determines whether you succeed or fail in life.

Many changes we need to make to become the person we're meant to be are *way* out of our comfort zones. So, it's natural to feel a little fear or an adrenaline rush as you try to stretch and grow. Remember how you felt when you first got into the swimming pool and didn't know how to swim? Or the first day of

> *Many changes we need to make to become the person we're meant to be are way out of our comfort zones.*

school? You probably felt some mixture of terrified and excited. But as kids, even though we were a little freaked out, we just kept trying new things, things we've never done before. We knew we'd be awkward at first but that didn't matter. We really wanted to grow and expand what we could do.

The thing about change is that it always offers you a choice. You can try to hide from it and resist it (which never works in the end because the change you need to make will catch up with you one day like a cosmic 2 X 4 that bashes you on the head!) or you can decide to step up to the plate and embrace it. You may not like the change, but you can still choose to use it as a launching pad into something bigger and better.

We've been successfully changing and taking tiny steps out of our comfort zones for our whole lives, hardly noticing it. All of us have changed our behavior or learned new skills to fit new situations since the day we were born. At one point, we decided we wanted to walk, right? So, we took a shot at it. I doubt any of us were great at it the first time around. But we didn't give up. We didn't sit back in our poopy diapers and say, "Wow. I better stick to crawling. It's much safer and I'm already good at it. I'm probably meant to be a crawler, not a walker. Walking is just too scary."

You've learned all kinds of skills over the years and navigated all kinds of new situations. You are a master of change. You've been an expert at change your whole life. You have proven over and over that taking those small steps out of your comfort zone did not kill you. And remember, we've already learned that you're at least as smart as a tree!

Your comfort zone also has a lot to do with risk and the Bad Wolf will tell you that taking risk is absolutely the last thing you should do! Risk means you can't guarantee the outcome—and the Bad Wolf will lie to you and make you think that *not* taking risks means you can guarantee what will happen to you. He's saying, "If I can get into your head, I will have you forever!" No, don't let him! Life comes with *absolutely no guarantees*! Staying in your comfort zone only guarantees that you'll miss all the good stuff waiting right outside of it. You won't apply for that great job or start that business. You won't ask that attractive person out for coffee or try that new sport you always wanted to try. Oh, you'll get to avoid feeling awkward and clumsy initially, and maybe dodge feeling some pain or embarrassment. But you'll miss out on all of the possibilities and opportunities out there too!

The Olympic gymnast Simone Biles said, "I'd rather regret the risks that didn't work out than the chances I didn't take at all." I'm with her! I've always believed Alfred Lord Tennyson's saying, "It's better to have loved and lost than never to have loved at all." Don't let risks stop you. What I've learned in my research is that the biggest regrets people have in life are the chances and opportunities that they didn't take that they know they could have.

Instead of thinking about the risks, you want to really think about the rewards. What will your life look like and feel like when you've moved out of your comfort zone to do the uncomfortable things that will get you where you want to go? What will your life look like and feel like once you've actually reached your goals and are in the middle of where you want to be? This is so important because the real reward, the true gold is not just because of the success you achieve. The true rewards are the satisfaction and joy you get from becoming a bigger version of yourself as you go after that success.

Fear of Failure

> *Think like a queen. A queen is not afraid to fail. Failure is another steppingstone to greatness.* —Oprah Winfrey

What about failure? The fear of failure is one of the Bad Wolf's best weapons to keep you in your comfort zone! One of the most common limiting beliefs that people have is about what failure means: "Failure is bad. Failure means you're not going to make it. Failure is a sign that you're a loser. Failure means you should give up."

For some reason, by the time we're adults, I'd say that too many of us see failure as a bad thing. We think it means that we're wrong or weak or dumb or incompetent. It means that we're on the wrong path and that we should give up trying to do whatever we're trying to do or trying to be who we're trying to become. We tell ourselves that if we've failed at something, it means we don't have enough talent or intelligence to do it. We *especially* don't want others to see us fail, to fall flat on our face in public. How embarrassing is that? So, we do everything in our power to avoid failure at all costs. And we feel this way about *everything*. We're afraid of failing in our relationships, as parents, in trying a new sport, beginning a new career, even in cooking dinner! So, we'll do *anything* to avoid experiencing failure.

But here's the problem with that:

"It is impossible to live without failing at something, unless you live so cautiously that you might as well not have lived at all, in which case you have failed by default." —J.K. Rowling

Oftentimes we use our past failures as an excuse. We quit trying to change our circumstance because we are afraid that we will fail again. I don't want you to see failure as bad. You're not tied to that string. You can cut it. You can chew at it until it breaks. You can yank your leg and pull the stake up. We can't be like elephants who once tried to break free and failed so never tried again. We've got to cut that string. We've got to keep trying. And, yes, we may fail along the way. But as long as we keep going, as long as we don't stop, we eventually will get where we want to be. Your history does not have to determine your destiny.

> Your history does not have to determine your destiny.

You know who doesn't hold limiting beliefs about failure? Highly successful people. Highly successful people have usually failed more times than they've succeeded. But that didn't stop them. They didn't shy away from failures. They used them as stepping-stones. The truth is that you need to fail time and time again to succeed at anything, especially when you're trying to make a change and go for something bigger than you've had before. When you're failing, it's a sign that you're moving in the right direction. It's a sign that you're actively pursuing your goal and eliminating what doesn't work. Successful people fail 11 times but then succeed twice. They are always 11 steps ahead of others going for the same goal because they risked being *wrong* to find out how to be *right*.

A friend and business partner of mine, Brent Gove basically graduated high school with such a low GPA that he did not get accepted into Chico State the first time he applied—which is a school that *anybody* can get into! He got denied *twice*. He ended up finally getting in after two rejections—and then he dropped out. He became a Realtor®. He tried to build a business and kept cold calling, getting hung up on, getting no's from thousands of people. But those no's didn't stop him. He kept his focus on the people who wanted to say yes. He kept pushing and moving forward. He lost a lot of deals but made tons of money because he worked harder than anyone else. And now he no longer sells real estate but joined eXp and built an enormous organization with agents across the nation and he crushes it! Today, at 54 years old, he makes over $1.1 million a month in residual income —all because he failed and never gave up. (Take that, Chico State!)

Years ago, when I started my real estate business, I knew I had to be innovative and creative and do things differently than everyone else was doing it. I had to step out and take some risks. And because I was doing things I'd never tried before, I knew I'd be making mistakes—sometimes big, fat, hairy expensive ones! This was even more true when I started my coaching business. Once I lost almost $900,000 in one month from changing something we had been doing. Obviously, I didn't like losing $900K and I had a moment of being upset, but I didn't sit with that moment for more than a few minutes. I made a choice, then I moved on and learned from it. What we changed clearly did *not* work but after the shock that this one change had cost me $900,000, I wasn't mad at all. My team was flabbergasted because every forecast we had showed we should have made $900K more. We didn't. I said, "Well, now we know what *not* to do." Then I focused on the good part of a change that we made. It was going to give me back about 22 hours per month of my time and also save my voice. Not what we'd planned, but still a good thing.

I can't even count the number of times I've totally bombed! It feels like my whole career path was by trial and error, sometimes with a big emphasis on error. But you know what? After every single one, I'd pick myself up, dust myself off, and start again. (Hey, but don't feel too bad for me because both of those ventures are now multi-million-dollar businesses!)

There's no way I could be where I am without all the stumbles and mistakes and failures I've had. And, if they're being honest, every single person who has made a significant change in their lives or who has become successful at something or who has lived a full and rich life will tell you the same thing. Failure is just part of the game.

No, I did *not* enjoy those failures! Some of them were downright painful and others were totally embarrassing. But I learned not to be so afraid of them. I learned to use them to my advantage and grow from them.

Failure does *not* define who you are. If you asked a little kid what failure is, they'd probably shrug and just say, "It's something you try that doesn't work out." But as adults, we think we should take failure personally, as if it's about who we *are*. No matter how many times you fail, it *isn't* who you are. Failure is just what happens on the road to something bigger.

And failure is *not* an enemy. People who are afraid of failure see it as a monster waiting just around the corner that is personally out to destroy them and ruin their lives. They seem to think that failure is bigger, stronger, and more powerful than they are. But failure isn't out to get you. It's neutral, just something that happens. And it isn't more powerful than you are. I believe we're never dealt a hand we weren't fully able to deal with, even if you don't know that at the time. The only way failure "wins" is if you fall down then don't get up to try again.

I always talk to my students about Ready, Aim, Fire! Many people spend so much time getting "ready" or trying to get the perfect aim that they never fire at all! You've got to fire, fire, fire! Take one deep breath to get ready, aim yourself at your target then fire! Don't waste your time trying to get the first two steps perfect. They never will be. You've got to go for it. My mentor and business partner with eXp Brent Gove always says "Get off of the couch and onto your feet!! Into the Battle and into the Heat!"

I know from my own experience that every failure can make you stronger and wiser. But this is only true *if* you take responsibility for it! If you blame your failures on someone or something else, you won't get the lessons. How about a little kid trying to eat with a spoon for the first time? It's a total mess, right? A lot more food ends up on the floor, in their hair and even their ears than in the kid's mouth! But as children, we all instinctively knew that it wasn't the spoon's fault. The spoon wasn't defective, and Mom didn't give us something that was impossible to eat with a spoon. We were smart enough to figure out that the spoon wasn't working because of *something we were doing or weren't doing*. It didn't mean we should give it up and eat with our fingers for the rest of our lives. Each time you flipped mashed bananas on your face, you learned how *not* to use that spoon. And you tried to do it differently. As adults, it's no different. Whenever you fail, you get to begin again but this time, you've got more knowledge and intelligence.

Failure is *not* a Stop Sign. This is SO important! Just like obstacles, a failure, even a big, fat, ugly, humiliating one (which we all have experienced), is *not* a sign that you should give up! When what you're doing doesn't work, it just means something needs to change. You might need to take a huge detour or maybe just make a small course correction.

I like the way that Tony Robbins talks about it. He says that there is no failure but only *results*. With that idea in mind, instead of getting all dramatic about blowing it, you can simply say, "Here's what we tried and here is the result we got. To get a different result, we need to approach it in a different way. End of story."

And most importantly, failing is better than regretting. There is a saying that the biggest regret is not changing something that you still can change. People find the most regret in life when they are at a point where they still *can* change something—but they don't. Look at your life: Where are you now? Do you have dreams of adventures, a new partner, or a new career that you haven't achieved? What's holding you back? Ask yourself if you still have time to make that change. Chances are you still can.

> People find the most regret in life when they are at a point where they still can change something—but they don't.

I can't even imagine where I would be right now if I'd quit any of my businesses after a few failures. Or, even worse, if I'd never tried at all and just stayed curled up in my comfort zone because I didn't want to "fail"! Personally, I think regret is one of the worst emotions ever. Yes, at times I was miserable when I completely flopped. But I got over it. And even if I hadn't attained the success I have, I know I'll *always* feel better about myself because I kept going.

So, paraphrasing Mr. Spock, may you "Fail big and prosper!"

Now I'm not saying that you intentionally go out and mess up, that you intentionally *try* to fail. What I'm saying is that you need to be willing to keep going and not get it right. Then keep going and make some more mistakes. Then keep going and fall short of your goal. Then keep going and try another way that doesn't quite work. And keep going.

You need to redefine failure for yourself to mean something positive. That's what successful people have done. They've made failure their friend. Like these people:

"Failure is simply the opportunity to begin again, this time more intelligently." Henry Ford (founder of the Ford Motor Company)

"Failure is another steppingstone to greatness." Oprah Winfrey

"A failure is not always a mistake, it may simply be the best one can do under the circumstances. The real mistake is to stop trying." B. F. Skinner (Harvard psychologist, author, inventor)

"There is no innovation and creativity without failure. Period." Brene Brown (best-selling author and research professor)

"The greatest glory in living lies not in never falling, but in rising every time we fall." Ralph Waldo Emerson (poet and philosopher who led the Transcendental movement)

Let me be really clear: The comfort zone is not your friend. Failure, and your willingness to change and take risks, is—because eventually you will succeed! So, stop telling yourself that change is so darn hard, risk is too scary, and that anything outside your comfort zone is beyond you! You've got this!

Expand Your Comfort Zone

Tony Robbins uses an exercise he calls "the Dickens" process after that book, *A Christmas Carol.* Remember how Scrooge was visited by all those ghosts? It was the ghost of Christmas future that really got to him, showing him how horrible his life would be if he stayed in his comfort zone, bah humbugging everything and being a cranky old miser.

Take out a piece of paper and first write what your life could look like if you do step outside of your comfort zone and do what you need to do to get what you really want. Get detailed and really think about all the rewards of that life. Then, on another sheet of paper, write down what your life would look like in 10 or 15 years if you stay in that comfort zone. Will you be in the same old life, with the same old problems and sense of unfulfillment? Or will the problems and unfulfillment be *even worse* now? Now think about being on your deathbed: How will you feel at that point knowing that you *could* have changed your life, but didn't?

Now that you have those images, it's time to use the Stop, Snap, and Do. Whenever you catch yourself retreating into your comfort zone, stop and give yourself a snap. When you transfer the band to the other side, bring up the positive image of where you will be by stepping out of your comfort zone. Or, if it's more motivating for you, bring up the image of where you'd end up if you stay there. Then take a step forward! Do something! Take some kind of action, some kind of risk even if it's very small, that pushes you out of your comfort zone.

Freezing at Obstacles

Another weapon the Bad Wolf uses to keep you in your comfort zone is to make you afraid of obstacles, that obstacles, like failure, mean that you shouldn't be doing what you're trying to do. I talked about false obstacles, the limiting beliefs we have about what we're capable of or how life works. We created them so we can get rid of them. But we also run into obstacles that we didn't create. We used to call obstacles "problems" until somebody thought it was way more positive to call them "challenges." (But when someone says, "We've got a challenge" you know they really mean problem, right? Yeah, me too.)

An obstacle is anything that seems to be in the way of you getting where you want to go. The goal is over there. You're over here. And between the two of you, there's some big, hairy thing or some tiny, squeaky thing in the way—an obstacle. When some people see an obstacle, they immediately think it's a stop sign or at least a sign that they're heading in the wrong direction. But it doesn't mean that. An obstacle is just something you need to learn to get over, under, around or through.

By the way, do you know what makes obstacles look huge? A very small vision. A small why. And you know what makes obstacles look tiny? A vision that is massive and a why that is totally compelling to you. (We'll talk about this more later in the book.)

Let me give you an example: Let's say you're sitting in a movie theater and suddenly you really need to pee (for most of us, that would be a compelling why!). You decide you need to go to the restroom (maybe not the biggest vision you've ever had, but majorly important in this very minute!). When you get up to move toward the bathroom, you're going to run into obstacles. You're going to have to climb your way over some people. You have to figure out where the heck the restroom is and maybe you'll have to wait in line. Now if you really, really need to pee, those obstacles will seem pretty minor. No way you're going to let them stop you, right? But if you really didn't have to pee that badly and you knew you could hold it, well, the obstacles might seem too difficult to bother with so you might just decide to stay put.

You need to treat *every* obstacle like you're going to do whatever it takes so you don't have to pee in your pants! There's *no way* you're going to let anything block you from your destination!

Hitting an obstacle on the way to your goal, on the way to changing what you want to change, just means that you're moving forward. It means that you're no longer just sitting around thinking, "It would be nice to make that change." It means you're actually up off your rear, moving forward and on your way! So, hitting an obstacle is a cause for celebration.

You've got to hear me on this: If you're *not* hitting obstacles, you don't have big enough dreams and goals. If your dreams are big enough and you're moving out of your comfort zone, you're absolutely going to run into hurdles along the way. If success in life was just easy peasy, *everyone* would be massively successful in every area of their lives. They aren't because they weren't willing to deal with the hurdles, challenges, obstacles and failures. They don't realize that those "difficulties" are really just how the universe is set up to help us learn about what does *not* work. Most obstacles show up to give you what you need to be successful. They either teach you something, help you make a slight course correction, or build some kind of strength in you.

> Most obstacles show up to give you what you need to be successful. They either teach you something, help you make a slight course correction, or build some kind of strength in you.

Obstacles are *not* there to punish you or discourage you no matter what the Bad Wolf tells you.

For example, one of my itsy bitsy obstacles to becoming the trainer, coach, and speaker I knew I wanted to be was that I was *scared to death of public speaking*. Just a minor obstacle, right? That I was terrified of doing the thing I most wanted to do.

It's true. Years ago in my real estate business, we'd all have to announce our listings to the other brokers on tour. I'd memorize everything I could about the house and mumble it to myself while I waited for my turn. When it was finally my turn, I'd be so frightened that I'd speak so fast that no one could understand me. I got so rattled that one time I even said my name wrong! I said "Krista Miller" (my previous married name) instead of "Krista Mashore." That's how freaked I was. But because I had that obstacle, that fear, I had to practice more and be better prepared. I had to reach out and get support and coaches. I had to reach deep down into myself and get stronger.

Today, I speak in front of thousands of people several times a year. I still get butterflies and I still even feel a bit of fear. But I continue to push through and, after I'm on stage for about 12-13 minutes, it feels fun and natural. But let me tell you I had to work and practice and fail and look stupid a lot of times before I was able to get there. You've got to push out of your comfort zone, and you can do anything. Each time I failed and made a mistake, I learned and grew from it. One time, my high heel got stuck on the stage and I fell! (Yep, that was embarrassing! And I've actually done that twice now!) Now I either wear different shoes or I take notice of where the stage joints meet where my shoe can get stuck. I didn't let that embarrassment stop me. Because I faced that obstacle, learned from it and became stronger, I know I'm a much better speaker than I would have been if I hadn't had that fear to overcome.

One thing that many people do wrong when they run into an obstacle is that they ask the wrong questions. When it hit me that I was terrified of the thing I wanted to do most in life, I could have asked, "How could I possibly have been so dumb to think I could do *that*?" That's the type of question the Bad Wolf loves and his answers wouldn't have been very helpful. Instead, I asked myself, "Okay, so what do I need to do now to get better at this?" The Good Wolf perked his ears up and gave me all kinds of ideas.

Our minds, especially our unconscious minds, are *so* smart! It doesn't matter what your IQ is, your brain is brilliant *if* you ask it the right questions. Lots of us don't use the full power of our brains because we ask all the wrong questions. It's like Google. You know how you plug certain words into the search box when you're looking for something? If you mess up and put in the wrong words or questions, Google takes what you gave it and finds the wrong thing for you. It's not Google's fault. Google did its job. But you sent it in the wrong direction.

Our unconscious minds are like that. When we're trying to solve something or get ideas to overcome an obstacle and we use the bad questions, we get the wrong answers, and the wrong situations present themselves to us. It's not our unconscious mind's fault. We sent it in the wrong direction by asking the wrong questions.

For example, let's say you're having financial difficulty. If you say, "How am I ever going to survive through the month?" your brain starts to work on "surviving through the month." It will help you re-member the dollar bill in your jeans, or it will make sure you see that discount coupon for eggs at the store. But when you ask a better ques-tion like, "How can I not only survive but thrive in the months ahead? Where are the areas of opportunity for me right now?" Whoa! Now your unconscious mind heads off in a totally new direction. It starts getting creative and new ideas pop into your head. It helps you notice and be aware of new opportunities. Its focus is what you asked for, helping you thrive, not just survive.

I remember back in the early days of the Covid pandemic, I heard people actually say, "What will I do when I run out of toilet paper?" Honestly, in my whole life, I've never had so many conversations about toilet paper as I had during those weeks! Anyway, when they plug that into their unconscious mind's search box, it's like the RAS (reticular activating system) says, "Okay, the idea is to run out of toilet paper and find something else. What else have we got lying around that we can use?" It doesn't even let them notice that Costco is stocked with tons of toilet paper right now.

A better question would have been, "What's the best way to find the toilet paper we need?" Now your mind focuses on, "Okay, best way to find toilet paper. How about online? How about hitting Costco early in the day? How about asking my neighbors if they've got extra right now? How about checking with that restaurant that closed to see if they have a stash?" It will literally come up with hundreds of ideas all about toilet paper! Not all of them will be good but some will.

A Better Question

Think of some of the challenges or obstacles in your life. What kinds of questions have you been asking about them? Can you start switching any negative limiting questions out to be better questions? Rather than, "What if I get laid off from my job?" ask, "If I get laid off, what even better opportunities are out there?" Instead of, "Why can't I lose these extra pounds?" try, "What's the best way for me to be the size I want to be?" Or take, "Why don't my kids ever clean their rooms?" and replace it with, "How can I motivate my kids to clean their rooms?" With better questions, you'll get much better ideas, and much better results.

One last thing that people often forget when they're hit with a challenge is "What do I *really* want from this? What's *really* important here?" When the recession hit and I knew my real estate career was in jeopardy, my goal was clear. I wanted to make enough money to stay in the business and support my daughters. I didn't care that my reputation became "The Foreclosure Queen" and some of the other agents made fun of me (though not for long!). I knew I was doing the best I could for the homeowners and the banks I served.

When a friend of mine was laid off from her high-powered, high-stress corporate job, she realized that she was on the verge of burnout and that the most important thing was to not let herself get so stressed and overworked again. Though she was offered other positions at the same company, she turned them down because her health was more important to her. When you know your ultimate goal and what you really want from a situation, you don't get distracted by the things that don't matter as much.

Change your attitude about obstacles! Despite what the Bad Wolf may try to tell you, obstacles are a positive sign and they are there to help you *if* you approach them right.

Conquering Obstacles

What's interesting is that the more you succeed, the bigger the problems and challenges become! The good news is that by the time you succeed, you're a heck of a lot better at dealing with them. Over the years, I've run into many bumps and potholes on the road, some minor, some pretty huge. But I've learned to take certain steps to face them:

#1 Mind your mindset: Decades ago, comedian Will Rogers said, "If you find yourself in a hole, the first thing to do is stop digging." Stop complaining about it and worrying about how it could get worse. Face whatever challenge it is like a superhero, like Batman facing the Joker or Luke Skywalker facing off with Darth Vader. Start with the attitude that nothing can defeat you and that there is a solution to this problem.

You need to get your head on straight! You'll need every ounce of your positive mindset to handle the difficult issue well, so don't come up with a bunch of solutions if you're feeling upset or fearful of whatever it is. Use your Stop, Snap and Switch. Tell yourself that you're stronger than any obstacle that could possibly come your way! Remind yourself that you're smart and capable and that you *will* find the best way forward!

#2 Be crystal clear about what you really want. So, if the result you *really* want is a team that is happy, loyal, and productive, the best solution probably isn't to rip somebody's head off because they messed up. If the result you *really* want is for your relationship to improve, your solution probably isn't to nitpick about your partner's tiny habits even though they are irritating. By knowing what you really want, you won't be tempted to overcome the problem by cutting off your nose to spite your face!

Some people try to solve challenges like they're playing "whack a mole." They find a quick solution for a small piece of the issue, but then other problems pop up. Some of the new problems that pop up are pieces their first solution didn't cover. Some of the new problems are actually issues that got created by the first solution! If you're crystal clear about the result you really want, you'll find solutions that don't cause other problems.

#3 Take whatever responsibility is yours. Even if you didn't directly cause the issue, is there some way you contributed to it? Did you not train that employee well enough or give them what they needed to succeed? Have you embarrassed your teenager in front of their friends so often that they don't want to confide in you anymore? Own up to whatever part of the challenge is yours.

#4 Ask the right questions. When everything hits the fan, people often ask questions that will *not* get them where they want to go. Questions like "Why does this always happen to me?" or "Why doesn't he love me as much as I love him?" are all questions that can't get you very far.

More Great Questions

To get the genius of your unconscious working on solutions, here are some questions that fit just about any challenge:

1. What are the important facts? How do I know they're the facts?

2. What do I think these facts mean? Could I interpret them a different way?

3. What can I learn from this? What is the gift in this, my gold nugget?

4. What can I change within myself to help solve or overcome this? What can I change in my *approach* to help solve or overcome this?

5. Who can help me with this?

6. What are some possible ways to solve this or overcome this? Which of these "fixes" keeps me moving in the direction of my goals?

7. What are the first steps I need to take? When will I take them?

Of this whole process, the most important step is the first one: being in a positive mindset. It will help you stay creative and solution-oriented rather than letting you get distracted by "Woe is me!" thinking.

Visit KristaMashore.com/SSSBook to get access to your Stop Snap & Switch resources

- Stop Snap & Switch Playbook
- Copies of graphics mentioned throughout the book
- Exclusive training videos
- 5 Day Limitless Life Challenge

SCAN ME

Your Limitless Abundance Map

"Nothing is impossible, the word itself says 'I'm possible'!"
—*Audrey Hepburn*

We've talked about where you've been and how it has shaped who you are—and that your history *doesn't* have to be your destiny. The first part of this book is about helping you recognize and destroy past negative thinking or limiting beliefs and mental junk habits from the past. But to get yourself moving forward, you have to know *who you really want to be*. You need to have a vision of the person you want to become, and what you really want to do and have in this life.

One thing that I've learned is that no one ever gets anywhere if they don't have a vision. I call it your Abundance Wealth Map. You can't get to Tuvalu if you don't have a vision of where Tuvalu is. (When you find out, let me know! It's supposed to be gorgeous!) You can't make a great New York style cheesecake if you don't have a vision of what it's supposed to look like or taste like. And you sure as heck can't create a great life for yourself if you don't know what that great life looks like either.

Most importantly, you need to know at the deepest level *why* you want that life. And you need to be clear that it fits your values because if you're not living up to your values, trust me, you'll never be happy no matter how bright and shiny your vision is. Your vision, your why, and your values are all tied so closely together! You can't really separate them, but we'll talk about them one by one.

Creating Your Vision

"If you don't like the road you're walking, start paving another one."
—Dolly Parton

I'm going to have you start with brainstorming what your perfect life looks like in all areas (then we'll dig deeper to create a vision that is totally compelling). If you haven't done a lot of visioning, or even if you have, I want you to follow some simple guidelines. (To see a video training and get guided through your Limitless Abundance Map, go to KristaMashore.com/SSSBook)

Creating Your Vision

#1 Don't analyze, brainstorm. This is just the beginning of the process so don't stress and try to get it absolutely perfect. We're not carving the Ten Commandments in stone here! We're just brainstorming to get our brains loosened up and flowing. Sometimes, it's like we're so busy just trying to handle life as it is, we forget to look up and see beyond what's right in front of us. So let yourself be creative and outrageous and dream big, *especially* in this first stage. We'll fine tune it as we go.

#2 Forget about impossible and reasonable. Remember who uses those words the most? The Bad Wolf! Plenty of people who are no smarter or stronger or better connected than you have done things that were supposed to be "impossible" and certainly seemed "unreasonable." So put a muzzle on that Bad Wolf! If others can do it, or have it, or be it, so can you—*with* the right mindset and a strong why!

#3 Create a vision in *all* areas. Life is not always balanced in every single moment. Sometimes you need to work harder on your career and other times you need to spend more time with your family. Sometimes you need to focus on your health and other times you need to pay attention to your personal development. That's okay, but if you get too far out of balance and *stay* there, something's going to break down. By including *all areas* of your life in your Limitless Abundance Map, you're less likely to let that happen.

#4 Make sure this vision is yours, not someone else's. Another person's vision of "the perfect life" is not necessarily yours! Make sure that your vision isn't based on what others want in life or, even worse, what others want *your* life to look like! Sometimes this is tough if parents or people around you have strong expectations about what you could or should be doing. Unfortunately, you can't muzzle them like the Bad Wolf! But you need to separate out what *they* want for you versus what *you* want if you want to be fulfilled and happy.

#5 Create it in the positive. We'll be using your vision to do visualizations and to let your unconscious mind know where you're headed. So, you don't want a vision that is "I don't want to be fat and out of shape." Your unconscious ends up with the picture of "fat and out of shape" and heads in that direction! Instead, you want to envision what you *do* want. Something like, "I'm a healthy size 8 and walk for 45 minutes every day. I work out 3 times per week. I have plenty of energy to do all I want to do. I look great and feel great!" What kind of picture does that give your unconscious to chew on? Much more inspiring, right?

#6 Don't get intimidated. Look, some people have these huge visions like "ending world hunger" or "winning an Oscar" or "becoming the number one player in the NBA" or "climbing Kilimanjaro." If that's what you want, more power to you! But if your vision is to have a happy, healthy family and work in a career you really enjoy, that's great too! Your vision doesn't have to shake up the world. It just has to be meaningful and inspiring to *you*. It has to fit *your* definition of true abundance for yourself.

#7 Make it a stretch for you. Even if your vision isn't huge and grandiose, it still needs to be a stretch, something you aspire to, that you'll have to grow into and get out of your comfort zone, something you'll have to work to accomplish. "Getting by" is not a vision. That's just the Bad Wolf talking. Be sure you're not playing too small with this.

#8 Don't worry about *how* you'll get there. For a lot of your vision, especially if it's a stretch, you may have absolutely no idea how the heck you're going to accomplish it! Don't worry about that. Highly successful people hardly *ever* know how to do what they envision at the beginning. They understand that the *how* will come if the vision is important enough. (Go to KristaMashore.com/SSSBook to view the training I did on the Limitless Abundance Map)

When I put together my personal Limitless Abundance Map in 2018, I had absolutely *no clue* how I was going to make it happen. Talk about a stretch! To go from zero coaching clients and no big speaking engagements to a multi-million dollar training business with hundreds of clients and speaking to audiences of thousands of people! My vision seemed huge and pretty farfetched. But my desire was strong to make it happen. Others had done it and I figured I could too. I look back and I've achieved everything on that Limitless Abundance Map—except for being a billionaire but I'm working on it!

For you to get started, take out your playbook to the Limitless Abundance Map page and you'll notice that you've got space for several different areas of your life. Having an awesome, abundant life is *not* just about having all the money and material stuff you want. That's part of it but real fulfillment is feeling rich in *all* areas of your life! I've listed the ones I use and also left space for "other" so you can tailor your vision to the way you think about your life. Here are the categories in the playbook with a short explanation:

Career/Vocation/Business: This is what you do for a living or the work that gives you the most satisfaction in life. For example, you may be an attorney, but you may get a lot of satisfaction from teaching at a community college as well. If you're retired, career/vocation might be volunteer work, a second career, mentoring or a serious hobby. (Since you're reading this book, I'm guessing that sitting around watching soap operas all day is *not* your idea of a great retirement!)

Family/Friends/Relationships: You might want to separate out friends, family, and your romantic relationship. Feel free to do that (and use the Other space if you need it). *All* relationships are important to a happy life! Think about the people you hang out with the most and all the people you connect with on a regular basis. Remember, they're the ones who have the most influence over you and your mindset and results. You don't need to include acquaintances or even distant family members if you hardly see them—*unless* that's something you want to change.

Money/Wealth: Don't skip this! Even if having lots of money isn't that important to you, your financial situation affects your ability to do or support the things that *are* important to you. So, you really need to include this in your Limitless Abundance Map. Your finances include income (from any source), investments, and savings. It also includes money you'd like to be able to give away as gifts or donations.

Health: Your health is a foundation for *everything* else you want in life. You don't need to be a tri-athlete or run marathons. But you do need to be healthy and energetic to support all of your other goals. You can't sacrifice your health for something else without paying a huge and ugly price!

Personal/Spiritual Growth I am a huge believer in constant learning and constant personal growth! I really think we've been put on this earth to become the best version of who we can be and that's a never-ending process. If you're not growing, you're dying. Your definition of "personal/spiritual growth" may be different than someone else's. That's fine, just make sure to include it if you really want a life that continues to be fulfilling and happy.

Contribution I also firmly believe that we each are meant to make our own, unique contribution to the world. This is where you'll think about what you have to offer and how you'd like to offer it. Again, your contribution doesn't have to be saving the planet. Maybe it's mentoring teens (one of my passions!) or taking care of elderly neighbors or volunteering at dog shelters.

Material Stuff We live in a material world (isn't there a song about that?) Having lots of material stuff may not be important to you but what would make you happy and support you in all other areas of your life? Your material stuff area might be "a car that's reliable" or a Lamborghini. The material stuff you want is unique to you. Don't judge yourself for wanting really expensive stuff—and don't judge yourself if you don't want it. Be sure to include services you want, like a full-time housekeeper or twice monthly massages.

Other Okay, this is, well, everything else! Put whatever you feel is left out that would complete your vision here. Or use this space to divide up another category. Maybe you want "travel and adventure" or "my home" as separate from material stuff. Maybe you want "education" to be separate from personal growth. Use this space to make your vision complete.

Create Your Limitless Abundance Map

Okay, so let me help you get started with some questions. First, rate your life just as it is today on your level of happiness and fulfillment in each category. Use a scale of one to ten. One means that your life in this area is just a little bit better than absolutely horrible. Ten means that your life is awesome in that area and you couldn't be any happier! (Hint: Most people are somewhere in the middle. And even if you're at a ten, what would make that category even *more* awesome?)

Next, start to brainstorm and write about what would make each area an absolute *ten*. If you could have your life be exactly like you want it to, how would it look? Try to be specific but don't stress over it. This is just the first step. What could you be, do or have in each area of life that would bring your level of satisfaction and happiness to a ten? Use the spaces on your Limitless Abundance Map page. Here are some questions to prompt you:

If you could have your dream job or business, what would you be doing? What career or vocation would make you so excited you could hardly wait to jump out of bed in the morning? What would inspire you so much that "work" hardly even felt like work? How much time would you spend at it? Where would you do it? Who would you do it with?

If you could have *all* the relationships in your life exactly as you want them, what would they look like? How would you and your partner be with each other and what would you share? What kind of connection would you have with your children and the rest of your family? Who would your friends be and how would you spend time together? What new friends would you have?

What would your financial picture look like? How much income would you have coming in every month or year? How much money would you have socked away? What kinds of investments would you have? How much money would you like to donate or gift to others every year?

In your perfect life, how would you feel physically? How much strength, flexibility, and energy would you have? What types of physical activities would you be doing? What would your body look like?

What kinds of things would you pursue to grow personally and professionally? What would you learn or study? What level of spiritual connection would you feel? What practices would you be doing? How would you feel emotionally and mentally? What kind of mindset would you have and how would you view yourself?

How would you contribute your gifts to the world? What organizations or groups would you support with your time, talent and treasure? What would you give back to individuals, your community or your world?

What awesome material stuff would you have? What does your dream home look like? Where would it be and what's in it? What type of car do you drive? What kinds of equipment or toys would you have? What would be in your closet? Would you collect something like art or antiques? What kinds of adventures will you go on? Where would you travel? What kinds of services (like a personal trainer or a life coach) would you have?

Now add anything else to this list that you could do, be or have that inspires you. If it doesn't fit under anything else, throw it into Other. Remember, it doesn't matter if you don't know how to accomplish what's on your list. It doesn't matter if it seems "unreasonable" or "impossible." When you work through the next section—knowing your why—you'll have the fuel you need to get you there.

> Are these exercises helping you to see a brighter future for yourself? If so, help me help others see a brighter future by leaving a review of my book on Amazon. Thank you!

Knowing Your Why

I've seen trainers teach about vision starting with, "What do you want your life to look like in all categories (financial, relationships, health, career, personal and spiritual growth, contribution)?" then move immediately to having students create vision boards, inspirational affirmations, etc. etc. Students come up with big fairytale *Lives of the Rich and Famous* visions that, when it comes down to it, they're not *committed* to working toward. It's a nice dream but not one that will get them up an hour earlier or make them sacrifice TV time. They might make a few puny efforts but then head back into their comfort zone at the first sign of disappointment or difficulty.

It's not that you can't have those things and have an awesome lifestyle. You absolutely can! But unless you're really *committed* to that vision and have a compelling reason for *why* you must have it or do it, you won't do what it takes to make it happen. (And if it doesn't fit with your values, you might get there but you'll be miserable.) You need to have a vision that, even if it looks totally out of reach, it's so exciting and compelling to you that you can *commit* to making it happen.

The reason that most people fail at achieving their goals and dreams is that they don't have a strong enough reason for achieving it! Like desperately needing to pee when you're sitting in the middle of a crowded movie theater, you'll climb over anything in your way to get to the bathroom. The *why* behind your vision has to be at the level of *burning desire*. You are so clear and passionate about *why* this vision *must* become manifest so that you will do whatever it takes. Some people call it "drive." Others call it "hunger" or "fire in the belly." Whatever you want to call it, that fire really has to be lit to keep you going through the ups and downs of getting to where you want to go.

Success isn't based on luck or having a faint desire. It's based on a burning motivation that keeps you on track when the luck has run out. If you don't know what your burning motivation is for going after your desire, that's okay, but you need to dig deeper. I say this from experience. At times in my real estate career, the market suddenly crashed, threatening everything I'd worked for. I had to pull up my big girl's pants and reinvent myself to keep it going. Because I knew my *why*, I didn't hesitate. I didn't just "try" to keep my business together. I was determined to "do" it. Starting my training and coaching business was no different. While I didn't have a clue what I was doing, I *did* have a strong sense of my purpose. It didn't matter that I made a ton of mistakes. My vision, my strong motivation kept me going.

How you will get where you want to go will show up if your *why* is strong enough. Reasons come first, answers come second. As Jim Rohn used to say, "If you *really* want to do something, you'll find a way. If you don't, you'll find an excuse." Your why is your main motivator.

Think about it. Is there something in your life today that once was a goal that seemed impossible, and you didn't know *how* or even *if* you could make it happen? We all have something like that that we've achieved if you really think about it. Maybe it was a car you wanted that seemed out of reach or a job you never thought you'd get. Maybe it's that special person you're with today that you never thought would ever notice you. Maybe it was a financial goal or graduating from college. Maybe at one time you never ever believed that you could actually learn to ride a bike! Whatever it is, at one time it seemed impossible, right? But now you've made it happen, even though you had no idea how to go about it.

To make that impossible thing a reality, at some point you decided, "This is what I want and I'm going to get there." You focused on it. You thought about it all the time. You got obsessed with it. Even though you didn't know how to afford that car, attract that person or ride that bike, you couldn't stop thinking about it. Your desire, your motivation, your why, was so strong that it tapped a potential in you. And that potential guided you to answers. You figured it out and didn't stop until it was done.

When you have that much desire, that much hunger, that much focus, your reticular activating system (your RAS) starts working for you. Remember that the RAS is the part of the brain that filters out non-useful information and directs your focus to helpful information. The RAS regulates what you notice, what you see and what you pay attention to. It's like when you're pregnant. You never noticed all those pregnant ladies around you but now they seem to be everywhere! That's because you've notified your RAS that now pregnancy is a big, important deal to you, so it starts pointing anything related to pregnancy out to you.

Carrot and the Stick

Everyone responds to two kinds of motivation: the carrot (something that gives you pleasure and makes you happy) and the stick (something that gives you pain and makes you miserable). Remember when we did the Dickens exercise about why you wanted to make some kind of change? It's the same with your goals and vision. It really helps if you can have both sides of your why: all the reasons why it will be beyond awesome to achieve that vision (carrot) *and* all the reasons it would be totally horrible if you don't achieve it (stick). This might sound overly dramatic, but if you think back to anything really big that you've accomplished in life, you can probably remember the big carrots and/or sticks that got you there.

My first real estate business was mainly built out of *desperation* (a stick) which is a super strong motivation and a very compelling why. This happened in 2003 on a Saturday morning. I was at breakfast with five of my girlfriends and all our kids. We had all gone to high school together and our children were growing up together. It was a perfect Saturday morning, laughing, reminiscing, kids running around playing. My phone rang and it was a friend of mine from college. She told me she had just seen my husband in Napa. I said, "Oh yes. He's there at a golf thing for work." She said, "No Krista, I'm so sorry but, I saw him being intimate with another woman."

My heart started pounding, my face got hot and flushed, my eyes instantly teared up. I felt like I'd been punched in the stomach with hurt and anger. My mind started racing in a crazy loop: "But, we have kids. We built this life together. How many more lies did he tell? How could he be so foolish to throw this all away?" Even worse, this was not the first time something like this had happened. I felt humiliated and angry at myself for "allowing" it to happen again.

I drove home, doing my best to hold back the tears so that my daughters couldn't see. And before I could even really wrap my mind around what was going on, I *knew* I was going to have to save myself. More importantly, I knew I was going to have to take care of my daughters and give them the life they deserved. I didn't know what that was going to look like or how I was going to do that. I had just left my safe, secure full-time job as a 3rd grade teacher to get into real estate. My plan was to work a less hectic, structured schedule so I could spend more time at home with my daughters. But now, that plan just flew out the window. I didn't have a Plan B and had no idea what to do next. But I remember a little voice inside saying, "You know Krista, your world is about to change drastically, and you need to be ready for it."

In an instant, my whole world turned upside down. I panicked thinking I might lose my daughters, or they might not be able to live with me. I was freaked thinking my kids could lose their home, that they'd lose any sense of normalcy being thrown back and forth between their father and me. My life got so crazy. Within a week of my husband leaving me and tearing up what I thought was our happy home (I guess we all think that our world is fine before it's torn apart!), I watched my two daughters being picked up by the new girlfriend who was driving my car! My bank accounts were completely drained, and we had just bought a new home. I mean who can even make up such a mess? Well, in a matter of days, this was my life.

Statistically, divorce is pretty common. Everyone seems to get divorced. It's normal, right? But it isn't normal for me, and it isn't normal in my family. My parents have been married for over 55 years and my brothers for 24 and 29 years. I think that made it even more devastating to me.

Yet in the midst of it all, I knew I needed to be able to support myself and my kids and give us a real life. It was up to me.

That realization propelled me into becoming the rookie of the year in my first year in real estate. It got me to work smart and hard, selling 69 homes my first year and averaging at least one hundred homes every single year thereafter. It was the motivation, the why, that built my business and put me in the top 1% of all Realtors® in the nation. Not because I wanted to. But I'd been thrown into survival mode.

That was the big, ugly stick that pushed me to do more than I ever thought I could. The carrot part was wanting to build a really positive environment for my daughters to grow up in. I had not lived at home since I was 13 so I felt I had missed out on something, and I didn't want them to miss out. The morning that the new girlfriend came and picked up my daughters driving my car, I sat in my kitchen drinking wine early in the morning (Don't judge me! It was a rough morning!) and staring at the backyard. We had just bought the home and moved in a few weeks before my husband and I split up, so we hadn't even landscaped the back. It was just dirt. I wanted to put flowers in the back. I wanted to build a playground and put in a pool so they could have their buddies over. I wanted that backyard to become a place where we could create great family memories. Even though I had that desire, I have to admit that the stick was probably stronger than the carrot at this time. Desperation can make people do all kinds of amazing things.

You often hear stories about mothers who somehow lift two-ton trucks off their child or run into burning buildings to save their baby. Those moms weren't necessarily naturally brave. They didn't run around every day in their Wonder Woman boots, and probably didn't have any kind of superhuman physical strength. But those moms were *desperate*. Those moms didn't just *want* to save their child. They knew that they *must* save their child. Their *desperation* to succeed and save their kid was so compelling that they went beyond anything they thought they could do. It was literally life or death to them.

A lot of motivational speakers tell the story of how Vikings used to burn their boats when they landed in a place that they planned to conquer. Doing this gave them *no choice* but to move forward and win. (Turns out the Vikings didn't do this but it's still a great analogy for creating a compelling why!) They couldn't just take a look at the enemy and say, "You know, conquering this place is going to be a lot harder than we thought. Let's get back on the boat and head home or maybe try someplace else that's easier." No, those guys either had to win or die right there. By burning their boats, they created some desperation and a very strong stick telling them why they *must* achieve their goal.

For most of us, the reason we want our vision is not usually a physical life or death situation. But it's often the *life or death of our dreams, our vision, our passion in life*. We're taught to focus on visualizing our vision and goals (and if you don't know how to do this, I'll show you later in the book) and how awesome it will be to achieve them. But how often do you stop to consider the *cost* of giving up or playing it small like we did in the Dickens exercise where we imagined where we'd be years from now if we didn't go for it? Because there always is a cost. It might be a tangible financial cost, the money you'll never make. It might be something tangible like you'll never have the family or the physical fitness you wanted. But it's more than that.

Every time you give up, every time you play small and back off, you chip away at who you are and who you were meant to be. You become less than who you really are. The more you do that, the more you feed the Bad Wolf. It becomes harder and harder to go for things that seem out of reach. It's a vicious cycle of mediocrity. You're reinforcing the neuropathways to *not* have the life you desire and deserve. Every time you retreat and feel sorry for yourself rather than try again, your dream or vision starts to fade. When you do that, you impact the people around you—your children, your friends, your co-workers. They watch you run away with your tail between your legs and think, "If he/she can't make it, I probably can't either." It has a huge ripple effect—and it's not a good one.

Every time you don't follow through, you deprive people who could really benefit from your gifts and talents. For me, I know I can positively impact others. I can help them achieve financial freedom and create the amazing life they desire. There are certain people that only I can reach. So, if I didn't do what I do, if I had backed off when I was scared or uncertain or tired, how many people *wouldn't* get those things because I wasn't there to encourage and inspire them? There are people that only *you* can impact. What happens to them if you give up?

That's why you need to find your compelling why! If right now you're feeling desperate to achieve your vision, start there. What are you *desperate* to change? What can you no longer stand in your life? What is *so painful* for you that you're willing to do *anything* to make it different? Maybe you've tried to lose weight before but then your doctor tells you that you'll die in the next three years if you don't lose some. Maybe your child needs a major operation that you need to pay for, and you don't have the money. Maybe you've gone through some horrible relationships and are desperate to make the next one better. Whatever it is, use that desperation, really tap into it, to blast you forward and help you achieve your vision for the future.

Even when it's built on desperation or the stick, remember that your vision can't be what you're moving away from like "not being fat" or "not being broke" or "not being lonely." What do you really *want?* Do you want to live long enough and be healthy so you get to do all the things on your bucket list? Do you want your child to have all that they need to get well and feel confident you can handle any future emergencies financially? Do you want to feel loved and cherished and safe with a new partner? Your compelling stick might be about feeling desperate about what you *don't* want. But your vision still must be what you *do* want.

A burning desire (as a carrot) can also be a really strong why. Unlike the desperation to build my first business, my second business was built from *inspiration* and *passion* which can be just as compelling. Over the years, I realized what I was passionate about: mentoring, teaching, and coaching others so they could find the success I had found.

In 2017, my real estate business was booming. In both terrible markets and great markets, I still figured out a way to succeed. I was remarried to Steve who is an awesome partner and soulmate. My girls were older and beginning their own lives. I was blissfully happy and grateful—*and* I also felt a nagging feeling that I was meant to do something more.

I absolutely love learning, so I had attended tons of workshops and seminars throughout my career (and still do). I learned a lot about everything from personal growth to success principles to specific marketing strategies. I knew these strategies and principles had contributed to the success I'd achieved. I'd passed them on to people I'd trained and mentored over the years and other people found them really useful too. I had picked up some really valuable insight, information, and wisdom, and I had seen for myself what a difference that could make.

I also have a passion for teaching and for giving back and helping others. It hit me that, by sharing what I know, I could help others succeed in achieving what they wanted in all areas of their lives. I could coach and train others so they could achieve the success they want to achieve in *all* areas of their lives. The inspiration, my compelling *why* for starting my coaching business was that passion for helping others. When you *know* you want to make others' lives better and you *know* that you have the tools to do it, how can you hold back?

Well, the truth was that I didn't have *all* the tools I needed. I had a lot to share but I was still terrified of public speaking. I didn't have a clue about how to build a coaching business. But I knew even then that how I was going to do it all didn't matter. Once you have a strong enough why, you can overcome and figure out anything! Seriously, if you get this step of uncovering your compelling reason *why* right, you're more than halfway there! When you're crystal clear on what really *motivates* you—your carrot and your stick—you'll find you can make the changes you need to make, to put the effort you need to put into it and blast through any obstacle that pops up. You'll stay on course and head toward the vision you've written on your Limitless Abundance Map because you know *why* it's so important.

Remember, your vision and your passion or purpose doesn't have to be some big earth-shattering thing, like ending all wars or finding the ultimate source of renewable energy. No! You can be passionate about providing an income to support your family and extended family. You can be passionate about writing romantic comedies or running a marathon one day. You'll know it's your true passion and vision when you feel fulfilled even before you get to "there" because you know you're taking steps toward it. You feel energized and excited and ready to throw your whole self into it! And that's how strong your why needs to feel.

So how do you find your why? Let's say that in your vision brainstorming, you wrote that you want to double your sales this year. Why? Because you want to make more money? No, that's not good enough. Do you honestly think you'd work that hard and make all the changes you need to make to double your sales just to see more zeros in your checking account? You need to go to the next level and ask, "Why is it important to make more money?" Maybe you want to upgrade to a nicer neighborhood. Okay, why is it important to you to live in a nicer neighborhood? Maybe because you want to send your kids to a good school. Well, why is it important for them to go to a good school? Maybe so they have opportunities and grow up as confident adults. Maybe because you'd feel safer if they were at a better school.

The thing is, you have to keep asking yourself "Why?" until you hit the motivation, the *why* that really hits a chord in you. It's got to be something that inspires you or that you're desperate to avoid.

Another example: Say you want to lose a few pounds. Now maybe that's easy for you but for some of us, it's like crossing the Pacific on a paddle board! It takes more motivation than "so I can button my jeans" to keep us from diving into a plate of nachos or a bowl of Chunky Monkey every night. So why is it important to lose a few pounds? Maybe it's to be healthier. Okay, why is it important for you to be healthier? Maybe so you can live longer. Okay, fine, then why is it important for you to live longer? Maybe it's so you can see your kids grow up and start families of their own. Maybe it's so you're around to play with your grandkids.

Okay, so now you've got a pretty strong reason to lose a few pounds. And I'm guessing if you keep that reason at the top of your mind, nachos and Chunky Monkey will seem much less important to you.

Seven Levels to Uncover Your Why

Look at what you've written on your Limitless Abundance Map so far and pick out a part of it that seems especially important or compelling to you. Write down *why* you want to achieve it, either using the carrot of something good about it or the stick of what you experience that you *don't* like because you *don't* have it.

Next, we're going to use the Seven Levels of Why that I learned from Dean Graziosi (who learned it from someone else). I'm honestly not sure why it's seven but whenever I use it myself or coach someone else to use it, seven seems to be the right number. Open your playbook to the Seven Levels of Why page and write down your first answer after Question #1: Why is achieving this part of your Limitless Abundance Map important to you? So maybe you have in your vision that you want to have your own business as a yoga instructor and your response to Question #1 is "Because I want to leave my job and I love yoga." You've got both a stick and a carrot. (You won't always have both in the beginning.) Question number # 2: Why is _____ so important to you? In this case, you'd fill in "leaving my job" and "teaching yoga" so the question would be "Why is leaving your job and teaching yoga so important to you?" Maybe you answer, "Because my job is exhausting, and teaching yoga makes me feel healthy and alive." Next, use that answer to fill in Question #3 so it reads, "Why is not being in a job that is exhausting and doing something that makes you feel healthy and alive so important to you?" Get the idea? Answer each question with your reasons from the last question then go deeper.

When you do this, you should end up with a reason why that makes you emotional. It's no longer just an idea of something that would be nice to have. You should start to feel really excited and inspired about having it, or maybe you really feel the painful cost of *not* having it.

Run this exercise with all of the main parts of your vision. It's kinda like flossing your teeth. My dentist always says, "You only need to floss the teeth you really want to keep." In achieving your Limitless Abundance Map, you only need to find your compelling why for the things you really want to achieve!

So, what happens if you really can't come up with a strong reason for something you've written in your vision? Well, you may need to tweak your vision or pull out the parts that are most motivating. For example, say you put that you want a $20MM dream house with tennis courts, a movie theater and a bowling alley. But when you really think about why you want that, it's to have a home that's mortgage-free where you can comfortably entertain your friends and extended family. You won't venture out of your comfort zone so you can buy a castle, but you'll do whatever it takes to have that comfortable, spacious mortgage-free home. And who knows? Maybe after you get that first home, the castle might make more sense to you in your next Limitless Abundance Map.

Now, let's talk about a final piece of your vision: your values.

Values

"Your core values act like the internal compass which navigates the course of your life. If you compromise your core values, you go nowhere."
—Roy T. Bennett

I have to admit, for a lot of my life I didn't spend too much time thinking about my values. It was important to me to always do the right thing, but I didn't bother trying to define specifically what that meant to me. And because I didn't define them, I made some decisions in the past I wouldn't make today. For example, I would not have married my first husband because family is a very important value to me. Even before we married, I didn't like the way he treated his family, especially his mom. If I'd really defined and honored my value of family, I would not have married him. (But then again, I got two awesome daughters out of it!)

As my mindset got stronger and healthier, I started to become aware of how immensely important defining what your values are and then living up to them is. It's not just a good idea. I know now that it's been a key to all the success I've had in different areas of my life.

Most of us have a gut feeling about what our most important values are even though we've never thought about them or can't really say what they are. When you're *not* living up to your values, you have that queasy feeling that you're doing something wrong. You might feel guilty or ashamed and like you'd be embarrassed to have anyone else know what you've done. Even if you can't put your finger on it, you feel like you aren't being true to yourself. When you're in conflict with one of your values, you feel stressed, and you just don't feel good about yourself.

Even though we have cultural norms of "good values" (in fact, there are some values that are almost universal throughout the entire world), everybody has their own unique personal values. A person's values aren't right or wrong, just different. (And if we all understood that, we would have a lot less conflict in the world!) Your particular values might be totally unconscious until you start to really think about them. You may not even know they're there until you're in a situation or forced to do something that runs against your values. That's when your gut will react.

Values are deeply-held beliefs that stay pretty constant over time. Your values aren't ideas you'd *like* to believe in. They're things that you deeply believe that you *need* in your life. They're your personal principles, your strong convictions, your unshakeable sense of right and wrong. That's why it feels so horrible when you go against them. When you aren't living up to your values, it's like losing a fundamental part of yourself.

And not living up to your values will always get you in the end! Think about Tiger Woods. Whether you like him or not, you have to admit he was on top of the golf world, almost unbeatable. Then what happened? As he himself admitted, "I stopped living according to my core values. I knew what I was doing was wrong but thought only about myself and thought I could get away with whatever I wanted to." Not only his career but his entire life fell apart because he stopped living up to his values. You can probably think of several other sports stars or entertainers or celebrities that followed a similar path. As soon as they went against the values that brought them to success, they fell apart.

Find out who you are and be that person. That's what your soul was put on this Earth to be. Find that truth, live that truth and everything else will come.
—*Ellen DeGeneres*

You can also think about people you know who have *not* denied their values, even after they became super-successful. Take Warren Buffet who is literally one of the wealthiest people on the planet. When talking about Mr. Buffet's core values, entrepreneur Josephine Geraci said, "Warren Buffett always lived within his means, never cared what other people thought about him, followed his gut and found his happiness in life's simple pleasures — family, a modest home and an honest living."

How about Oprah Winfrey? If you know anything about her (and who doesn't?!?), you know that values like generosity, compassion, and a strong work ethic show up in everything she does. She has often talked about how her huge success was based on staying true to her principles. When she was making a presentation to a crowd of Stanford Graduate Business School students, she said "If I were to put it in business terms or to leave you with a message, the truth is I have from the very beginning listened to my instincts. All of my best decisions in life have come because I was attuned to what really felt like the next right move for me." At another time, she wrote, "Leadership is about empathy. It is about having the ability to relate to and connect with people for the purpose of inspiring and empowering their lives."

Our values are there whether we're conscious of them or not. But the great thing about knowing what they are *consciously* is that they can guide you to make much better decisions in your life and avoid disasters. For example, think about choosing a career. If you know that you really value security and stability, then maybe a career in government or a job in the medical profession is right for you. But if you really value independence and creativity, those careers could be miserable for you, and you'd do better in a career like graphic design or architecture. If one of your core values is spending time with your children, you need to reconsider whether being a chef on a cruise line is a good option for you. What about relationships? If you really value fun and excitement, you probably won't do well with a partner who mainly values solitude and calm. What about the kind of company you go to work for? If you value individual achievement, you probably won't enjoy a company that's big on teamwork and collaboration. How much better would it be to *know* your values *before* you leap into these situations?

Discovering your values and living up to them is one of the most powerful tools in your toolbox to help you become the person you want to be and to live the life you want to live. Staying in alignment with your values is absolutely necessary if you want a life that is happy, fulfilling and satisfying.

Knowing your values gives you a sense of purpose and a map for your life. They keep us on track and make it easy to spot the off-ramps that we *don't* want to take, no matter how attractive those off-ramps might look at the time.

That's why it's important to spend time uncovering your values and making sure that everything in your vision is in alignment with them. If your vision includes backpacking to exotic places but one of your core values is safety, you may need to reconsider your travel plans. If in your vision, you've put down that you want to own a fleet of Hummers and one of your main values is "protect the planet," you may need to make sure those Hummers are the fully electric model!

Let me share a couple of personal stories about how my values impacted my success and the decisions I've made pursuing my vision.

My goal for years and the vision in my manifesto (which we'll talk about in the next section) was to be speaking on stages across the country to thousands of people. I had done that, but my team really, really wanted me to get on stage with a certain high-powered speaker that we'll call Mr. X. Finally, the opportunity came up and an organization asked if I would speak on a panel. Mr. X was speaking on stage at the event, so I said, "Sure, I'll absolutely do it." I had said yes before I really knew a whole lot about the event itself. I wasn't going to be a main speaker, but I didn't care about that. I was just happy to be invited.

When I finally checked out the lineup of speakers, it was all men. Twelve male speakers and not one woman. In addition, there was only one African American man speaking. All these high-powered white men looked like a meeting of the Ku Klux Klan. It really rubbed me the wrong way. I just got this really ugly feeling.

So, I told my team, "Look, team, I know you worked hard to get this opportunity for me to share the stage with Mr. X. But I'm not going to be on this panel. The speakers' line up is all male and I just don't want to be promoting an event that doesn't feature any women." They were stunned and said, "Okay but can we just—" I cut them off. "But nothing. I cannot do it." I've never considered myself a big feminist. That said, I really believe in the potential of women and feel strongly about supporting them.

I sent an email to the host organization and said, "Hey, I know I said that I'd be on this panel. I don't want to go against what I had said, but I didn't really look into it. When I went to your page, I noticed that it was all men and only one African American. It looked like a sausage festival. Real estate is 65% women, and my clientele is 70% women. You want me to promote this thing to my audience and I don't feel right about doing it considering the way it looks.

I went to the event website, and it made me feel yucky. I wish you all the best, but I'm going to respectfully decline being on that stage. If I can give you any advice at all, as a master at digital marketing who analyzes marketing and results, I'm telling you that you are losing people. Because if I felt this way going to this page, I can guarantee you that every other woman that went there did as well."

They responded back and said, "Krista, you're going to do great, and we promise we'll get more women. Please, if you can just do it. You said you would." And because I had said I would, I told them I would go ahead and be on the panel. But I let them know that I still didn't feel right about it. So, they made me a speaker, which didn't make a difference to me. I wrote back and said, "Look, I don't care if I'm a speaker but here's an easy fix. Take 10 minutes away from every male speaker and get more women up there. It looks weird having no women." And they got several new women to be speakers as well. Then they made me a keynote speaker, so I was going to be on the stage with Mr. X after all. But this time, I'd be feeling great about it! By saying no and living up to my principles, and my values, and my ethics, it ended up being a really good thing. They ended up totally revamping the whole event.

When I told my daughter what had happened, she literally cried. "Mom, oh my God. That makes me feel so proud that you did that."

Even though it meant risking a great opportunity, I didn't let my conscience take a back seat. I did what I felt was right. And the reason this decision was so clear and easy to make was that I *hadn't* stayed totally true to my values the year before—and I never wanted to feel that way again.

That situation the year before had to do with someone in my mastermind group who asked me to partner with him on some trainings. I felt hesitant but agreed. As soon as we started working together, I knew I shouldn't have said yes. I hated how he treated me and other women. After a few months, I told him that I wasn't going to continue our partnership.

While we were still working together, he had been flying to my events to watch me run them. He ended up literally taking my entire strategy of what I teach and how I do it. He took what I had created over the prior eight months and basically said that it was his. I confronted him and he told me it was a mistake, that he'd created those materials when we were still partnered.

When I approached the mastermind organization, they had a lot going on and didn't want to deal with it. They said, "Hey, we don't want to get involved. If you guys can't figure this out, you're both just going to have to leave the mastermind. But if you can just get along, you can stay." They got us on a Zoom call together. And I felt him being verbally demeaning to me again. Nothing had changed about who he was and how he was dealing with this situation. I felt yucky again.

And here's where I let myself down. I just let it happen. I let him talk down to me. I was afraid that if I left the mastermind group, it might look like I had done something wrong. I sat there thinking, "I feel horrible. This is so against my principles. This guy is dishonest and quite frankly harmful. He could be hurting the mastermind." Even thinking that, I was still more concerned about what other people would think.

So, I stayed in the group feeling horrible and knowing I shouldn't have stayed. Several people in the mastermind told me that he was bad mouthing me behind my back. He even said he had hired an attorney and taken out a Cease and Desist order against me! (Which was not true.) After about a month, I'd had enough. This guy continued to tell lies and be deceitful. At that point, I said, "You know what? I'm done. I'm leaving the mastermind. What other people think is not my problem." And I left.

That's when everything started turning around. The mastermind organizers called and said, "Hey, we don't want to see you leave. We don't want to lose you. We think you're a great value and asset. Would you be willing to go to our highest, highest level of mastermind? Then you won't need to be around that person." This higher level mastermind had no openings. It had a waiting list. But they were so determined to keep me that they made room for me anyway.

I made a decision within a two-hour timeframe. I booked my flight to Idaho that evening to attend this new higher-level mastermind group. I made the investment of $150,000 and jumped on a plane the next day because "Money likes speed and action takers are money makers." Within just a few months, being in that group and making that investment had paid off a hundredfold.

You can never go wrong by sticking to your principles and staying true to your values. You can never go wrong by doing the right thing. As scary as it might be sometimes, the Universe always finds a way to reward you for it.

Identify Your Values

You may be pretty clear about some of your values already. If so, go to your playbook and start writing them on the long list of values. Remember, these are not things or qualities that you *wish* you valued or you think you *should* value. It's what you honestly feel is important. In other words, if everything else was great but this thing was missing, you would *not* be happy. Like that conference I was asked to speak at. It was awesome that I finally got to be on stage with Mr. X, *except* there were no women represented. So, I didn't feel great about it—I felt horrible!

Start by brainstorming your values. To get you started, think about times you were really proud of yourself or happy about something you'd done. What was it about that that made you feel good? What quality or value did it show? You can also think of times when you were disappointed in yourself. Don't feel bad, we've all had them! What about that didn't feel good to you? What value or principle were you going against? (And if you need some inspiration, we've included a list of qualities for you to think about in the playbook.)

When you have a pretty good long list, go to the next list. We're going to narrow your list down to your most important, core values. If you only got to pick 10 of the values you listed, which would they be? (Notice that some of your values may be similar, like kindness and compassion. If they feel the same to you, you can combine them into one.) Of this top ten list, highlight the ones that feel the most important to you. Not just the "nice to have" but the "absolutely must have" values. In other words, if you had a boss who was a slob and you value cleanliness, you might be okay with that. But if you value respect and had a boss who was abusive to you and your co-workers, that might be a deal killer.

Now look back at the Limitless Abundance Map you started while keeping in mind the values you highlighted. Does everything in your vision line up with your values? Take a serious look at anything in your vision that runs against your values. I can't tell you what to do. But I can almost guarantee that when —or *if*—you make that part of the Limitless Abundance Map happen, it will *not* make you happy or fulfilled. (I threw in *if* because often if something goes against your values, you'll unconsciously sabotage your efforts to get it.) Is there a way you could tweak your vision so it does match your values? Do you need to add something to your vision to make sure certain values get more attention?

Now that you've matched values to your vision, we're ready to put it into the tools that will help you achieve it!

Here are some values to help you think about this. You'll find this list in your Limitless Abundance Playbook as well:

achievement	dependability	inner strength	reliability
adaptability	development	innovation	resourcefulness
adventure	devotion	integrity	respect
accountability	dignity	intelligence	responsibility
appreciation	efficiency	intuition	security
authenticity	empathy	kindness	sense of purpose
balance	empowerment	knowledge	service
beauty	environmental awareness	learning	sharing
being valued	equality	listening	spirituality
belonging	excellence	love	stability
calmness	exploration	loyalty	success
caring	expression	making a difference	supporting others
challenge	fairness	nature	teamwork
cleanliness	family	non-violence	tolerance
collaboration	forgiveness	obedience/duty	transparency
commitment	freedom	openness/honesty	trust
common sense	friendship	order/control	truth
community	frugality	patience	uniqueness
compassion	fun	patriotism	variety
competence	generosity	peace	wellbeing
connection	gratitude	perseverance	wisdom
contribution	growth	positive attitude	
cooperation	happiness	pride	
courage	health	productivity	
creativity	harmony	professionalism	
curiosity	helpfulness	protection	
	honesty	playbook	

Habits, Rituals and Tools to Achieve Your Limitless Abundance

Your beliefs become your thoughts. Your thoughts become your words. Your words become your actions. Your actions become your habits. Your habits become your values. Your values become your destiny. —Mahatma Gandhi

Your beliefs become your thoughts. Your thoughts become your words. Your words become your actions. Your actions become your habits. Your habits become your values. Your values become your destiny. — Mahatma Gandhi

(I say, "Your thoughts turn into your actions which make up your life." Same thing but a bit simpler lol!)

You've written down what your perfect life looks like. Now you need to develop the mindset, the belief and the certainty, that will get you there. A lot of what we've talked about so far is about the *general* mindset you need to succeed at anything. Now it's time to direct your mind to the specific type of success you're looking for. To do that, you need to bring some *new* habits and rituals into your daily life. Your old habits and rituals (like bingeing on negative news, constantly reliving past disappointments, hiding out in your comfort zone, etc.) have gotten you to where you are today. So, unless you're at a 10 in all areas of your life right now, you need to adopt different habits and rituals to get you where you want to be. These new habits are so simple. And once you do them enough, they will start to become a positive addiction.

I'm going to share some of the tools I've learned and some I've created that I *know* can support you in achieving your Limitless Abundance Map. How do I know? Because I've used them myself to achieve my dreams and I've watched hundreds of my students do the same. The goal of these tools is to bring you to "unconscious competence."

In learning anything, you go through 4 stages. This comes from Noel Burch's Hierarchy of Competence. First there's unconscious incompetence. You totally suck at something, but you don't know it! Maybe you suck as a guest in someone's home, or you suck at delegating to the people who work for you. But unless someone points it out, you have no idea that you suck. Another example: A lot of people are horrible about keeping commitments, especially to themselves. They say they're going to do something then they don't. They may start the day saying, "You know what, I'm going to really watch what I eat today and get in some more exercise." Then they inhale a Snickers or two after lunch and blow off the gym to grab some sliders and brewskies with a buddy after work.

The biggest lie that you can tell is the lie that you tell yourself. Anytime that you commit to doing something or say you'll do something and you don't do it, it's like you're lying to yourself. You keep letting yourself down and then you lack the self-confidence and initiative to try and venture out. You are self-sabotaging yourself each and every time you let yourself down. The sad thing in the example above is that they don't even *notice* the damage they just did to their own belief in themselves. They don't even realize that they suck at keeping their commitments. That's "unconscious incompetence."

The next stage is "conscious incompetence." You still suck at something but now you know it! You know you're horrible at talking to someone you're attracted to, or you know you suck at picking out clothes that look good on you. You know it, but you still suck at it. In the commitment example, this is when you realize, "Yikes! I keep saying I'll eat better and exercise, but I don't." Unfortunately, most people use this new awareness to start beating themselves up and feeling bad about themselves. Instead, what you want to do is move to "conscious competence."

Conscious competence is when you're working to get better at whatever you sucked at. You not only know you have a problem but you're working on solutions. Maybe you're getting coaching from an expert or practicing with a friend or taking lessons in whatever it is that you sucked at. Maybe you're adopting new habits and rituals and using new tools. In the commitment example, maybe you decided, "Okay, I'm at least going to write down everything I eat so that I'm more aware of it. And I'm going to park far away from the office and walk up the stairs at work rather than taking the elevator." Every time you have to remind yourself to do it until it becomes natural. When it finally becomes natural, you're at "unconscious competence."

The conscious competence stage is the hard part. When you're learning something new or trying to make changes, it's challenging. It doesn't usually come easy. It takes time, energy, and resources when you're trying to learn new habits or unlearn habits and routines that were not serving you well. When you're trying to get into a healthier routine for example, you'll get sore from working out. You might crave sugar or caffeine and get grouchy and irritable because your body is not used to this new routine yet.

When my students are first learning to use digital marketing and video, they suck at recording them. They're nervous and make a lot of mistakes and worry about what they look like or sound like. They get frustrated because they're learning a new skill and not catching on quickly. This is the danger zone where they get tempted to give up and go back to their old way of marketing. They know that the old way is inefficient and ineffective, but it's easier because it's familiar. But when you put the work in and push through the discomfort, push through the learning curve, you end up with a new skill or competence that becomes easy and almost effortless. That's when it's turned into unconscious competence or mastery.

When you think of unconscious competence, think of Oprah Winfrey interviewing someone or Kobe Bryant shooting at a basketball hoop. They don't even think about it. They just naturally do an excellent job. But you know how they got there? Because *they focused on the conscious competence* stage. They pushed through the hard times. They fumbled and fell and got back up. Oftentimes during the conscious competence stage, we get worse before we get better. Our results when learning something new aren't as good as the results we got with the "old way". Whenever a golfer tries to change and improve her golf swing or a musician tries a new fingering technique, the results are worse at first. But by pushing through until mastery, they finally experience how much more powerful the new way is.

The masters like Oprah and Kobe that we see around us practiced and got feedback and learned until they were naturally amazing. They adopted new habits and rituals in their daily lives that supported what they were doing. And they kept up with these new routines. For example, as good as he was, Kobe Bryant used to train for 6 hours per day in the off-season. Then before every game, he'd show up four hours early and shoot hundreds of shots. He was keeping his unconscious competence sharp by practicing conscious competence.

And that's what you'll need to do. Fortunately, it's a heck of a lot easier than Kobe Bryant's training schedule!

The basic ritual I teach all my students is a simple ritual that you do every morning and every evening. It just takes about 7 minutes and most if it is on one sheet of paper. Before I show you the template, let's break down the parts of it:

Manifesto

One of the tools for manifesting your Limitless Abundance Map is your manifesto. A manifesto is a written declaration of your intentions, motives, commitments, and ultimate vision. It will not have every tiny detail of your Limitless Abundance Map. It will be short, no more than one page, and it will include all the important themes or ideas that are the basis of your map. It's based on your passion and purpose, your goals and your values.

A manifesto isn't something you write down once then forget about. I tell my students to read it once in the morning and once at bedtime. I also have them read it when they're feeling down or before any important event or appointment where they want to show up as their best. In fact, it's best if you memorize it and if you read it often enough you naturally will memorize it. You want your manifesto to become so much a part of you that it's like your default switch. Whenever something comes up, your mind will instantly go to your manifesto. It will help guide all of your decisions and keep you connected to what is truly important to you when everything hits the fan.

My manifesto is one page, and it covers all aspects of my life: family, health, my relationship, business, and my community. It's in present tense and positive. I wrote it in 2018 and still repeat it to myself every morning and every night. I have copies of it in color in my office and my bedroom as a constant reminder of what I'm about:

I am a loving, loyal, supportive wife, mother, employer and friend. I am a philanthropist. I am the number one trainer in the world. I speak at conferences across the country. I have trainings with thousands of people. I am a leader. I positively affect every life that I touch. I make a difference in the world. I uplift and upbuild those around me. I help others achieve more in life and have more financial freedom and time. I am building Community Market Leaders© across the country who make an impact in their communities & who are go givers. I am a billion dollar company.

Except for the billion dollar company—I'm still working on it!—all of the rest of it is true today. When I wrote that in 2018, I had never spoken in front of anybody. I'm the person that would get on tour and literally forget my name. When I was on brokers' tour, getting up in front of 50 people to talk about my property, I said the wrong bathrooms, the wrong bedrooms and my wrong name because I was so nervous about it. So, for me to speak in front of thousands of people and to have that goal, was a huge stretch. I wrote it because I truly believe that I was built on this earth to make an impact. I believe that God or the Universe (insert whatever you call your higher power here!) put me here to help people and to get them to take action and to just have a positive life. I'm a catalyst for that. And this manifesto kept me inspired and on track.

Here's another example:

I am a dynamic, creative business owner and marketer. I give all my clients incredible value and stay on the cutting edge of my industry. I am dedicated to the success of each and every member of my team. As dedicated as I am to my business, my wife and children always come first. I schedule my work around events that are important to us as a family. I give generously of my time, talent, and treasure to the causes that I believe in. To do all that I want to do, I stay committed to taking care of my health: body, mind and spirit. (To see a copy of this manifesto and a few others, go to KristaMashore.com/SSSBook).

Now it's your turn. Review your Limitless Abundance Map and think about the main ideas behind it and the things that are most important to you. Then come up with a sentence or two that gets to the heart of it for each area. For example, in the manifesto, you don't need to say, "I attend every school play and coach my son's Little League team and my daughter's soccer team and I help them with their schoolwork and celebrate their birthdays and take my wife out on her birthday…" Just saying that your family comes first and you schedule yourself so you can participate is enough. You'll know what you mean by it. And remember, your goal is to memorize your manifesto! You'll be saying it out loud to yourself every morning and every evening and any time you need to feel your Superman/Superwoman energy.

Creating Certainty

Remember that Tony Robbins' Success Cycle from introduction? Where your certainty/belief feeds into how you tap your potential which controls how strong your actions will be which determines your results. So, to achieve the success you

> *You create certainty by getting the results you want in advance in your mind. And you do that through visualization.*

want in any area of your life, it's important to start with certainty and belief. We've been working on getting rid of those negative beliefs that have held you back. Now you need to create *absolute certainty and belief that you can achieve what you want.* "Wait! If I haven't achieved success in the past, how the heck can I be certain that I will now?" You create certainty by getting the results you want *in advance in your mind.* And you do that through visualization.

When I start talking about visualization, some of my students roll their eyes. They still think of it as some airy fairy New Age thing that people use to try and win the lottery. It's not. Now that scientists can watch the brain in action, they've learned a lot about how visualization and affirmation works.

Research has shown that visualization actually fires up the same parts of the brain in the same way as physically doing something. The brain doesn't seem to know the difference between actually doing something and just thinking about it. So just using your imagination alone strengthens the neural pathways involved in whatever activity you are visualizing.[4] You are literally training your brain, just in the way you would train a muscle. When you visualize something over and over, it lights up your nervous system and gives it "practice" in doing whatever you're visualizing.

Let me give you a taste of how it works. Stand up and stand with your feet about shoulder width apart. Now reach down toward your toes and go as far as it is comfortable for you to go. Then stand up and do it again, still just reaching as far as comfortable. Now stand up and *visualize* reaching down and touching your toes smoothly then visualize yourself comfortably and effortlessly bending farther until your palms and maybe even your forearms are on the floor. As you visualize this, feel it in your body as if you're actually doing it but don't move. Then visualize yourself standing back up again taking a deep breath. Do it again, visualizing bending down to the floor again and touching the floor with your palms or forearms with no effort at all. And it feels natural and you're having fun and you expect to touch the floor. Repeat this a couple more times. Next, open your eyes and *physically* bend down toward the floor, again without straining. Notice how far you are able to go down now.

Did you go farther than the first time? If you really did the visualization, your answer has to be "yes." Maybe you didn't get all the way down to the floor, but you were still able to bend down farther comfortably after visualizing that you could. It wasn't about stretching your physical body. It was about *stretching your mind* to accept a new and better result than you thought you could do! That's what visualizing your success is all about.

Couldn't you have reached further down to the floor than the first time? Could you have gone as far to the floor the very first time as you did the second time after visualizing it? Of

> The point is that you can have the best plan in the world and all that you need to get what you want, but if you don't have the belief and the certainty that you'll succeed, somewhere along the way you'll give up or back off.

---

4   Decety & Grèzes, 1999: https://pubmed.ncbi.nlm.nih.gov/10322473/

course, you could! But you *didn't* because you have a set of beliefs and
a certainty about how far you can bend to the ground. We have limiting
beliefs about absolutely everything, and we don't even realize many of
them. The point is that you can have the best plan in the world and all
that you need to get what you want, but if you don't have the belief
and the certainty that you'll succeed, somewhere along the way you'll
give up or back off. Or even worse, you won't try at all.

To build that certainty in your mind, you need to keep seeing your
results in advance in your mind. You need to visualize your successful
achievement vividly, feeling it as if it was happening right now, over
and over. It's not enough to visualize it once or twice. To get those new
neuropathways in place, to get your RAS working toward your desire,
you need to repeat it consistently until it becomes part of you.

The truth is that we use visualization all the time without even noticing it! Have you ever worried about something? Of course, you have!
We all have, right? That's you visualizing or imagining that something
in the future is *not* going to turn out well. For example, say you're afraid
of public speaking like I was. I'm betting that every time you worried
about doing it, you imagined yourself feeling nervous, maybe even
having a total brain-freeze and forgetting what you're supposed to say!
As you imagined that horrible result, you probably felt it in your body
and in your emotions. The problem is that when you're remembering
past failures or worrying that you're going to fail again in the future,
that's the neuropathway you're strengthening. The brain reacts just the
same whether it's in your imagination or actually happening. You are
actually rehearsing to fail! If you want something different than what
you have today, you need to turn that around and rehearse success.
Whenever you start imagining that you won't succeed, you need to
Stop, Snap and See yourself being *successful* so that the neuropathway
of success is strengthened instead.

I saw a YouTube video that talked about Dr. Judd Biasiotto and his
experiment using visualization and basketball. Dr. Biasiotto split people randomly into three groups and had them throw a bunch of free
throws to see how many they typically could make. Then for a month,
he had the first group practice free throws physically every day for an
hour. The second group just visualized themselves making free throws
without doing any physical practice. The third group did nothing.

After 30 days, he tested the groups again. The group that did nothing at all improved 0% (surprise, surprise!). The group that did daily physical practice (they actually threw the ball) improved by 24%. The visualization group improved by 23% without even touching a basketball for a month! I tried to verify the study and statistics but couldn't. But here is some research I could verify:

Researchers at the Cleveland Clinic Foundation in Ohio decided to see whether visualization could actually build muscles. They took 30 healthy young adults, tested their muscle strength then split them randomly into 3 groups. Group #1 was supposed to visualize exercising their little pinkie finger muscles for 15 minutes per day, 5 days a week for 12 weeks. Group #2 was told to visualize exercising their biceps for the same amount of time. Both of the groups were told to make the imaginary muscle movement *as real as possible* without actually moving that muscle. During that same 12 weeks, Group #3 didn't do any visualization or physical training at all.

After 12 weeks, Group #1 increased the strength in their little fingers by 53%! Group #2 increased their strength in their biceps by 13.4%. (Group #3 had no change—surprise, surprise!). What the researchers concluded is that visualization had actually trained their brains and improved their brains' ability to signal muscles![5] But based on other research I've read, I'm pretty sure they would have gotten even stronger if they had done the visualization *and* physically exercised those muscles (though I'm not sure why anyone would want a super-powered pinkie!)

For example, back in 1989, Lori Ansbach Eckert wrote a master's thesis titled: *The Effects of Mental Imagery on Free Throw Performance.* She wanted to explore which would improve performance more: visualization alone, physical practice alone, or practice combined with visualization. She randomly chose 120 college PE students and divided them into 4 groups: Group #1 did only visualization of free throws, #2 only practiced free throws physically, #3 practiced physically *and* did visualization, and #4 didn't do anything but watch basketball games. She had them all shoot 20 free throws at the beginning of the study to get a baseline then again after 5 sessions so she could check for improve-

5   https://www.verywellfit.com/can-you-build-strength-with-visualization-exercises-3120698

ment. Both Group #1 and #2 improved more than Group #4 (the couch potatoes). But #3, the group that did both physical practice and visualization did *significantly better* than any of the groups.[6]

The point here is that you can't expect to sit in your Barcalounger eating nachos and imagining wonderful things happening to you. You need to take action and work toward it. But *just* working hard is like just physical practice. You'll get much farther much faster by doing both! When your mind becomes *so certain* that you can and will achieve what you want, it steps right up to help. The opposite is true too: If your mind is convinced you *can't* make it happen or even just doubtful, it will throw all kinds of problems in your way.

Sara Blakey is the founder of Spanx and the world's youngest self-made billionaire. She started out with just $5,000 and an idea. She also had learned about visualization when she was just 16 from some Wayne Dyer cassette tapes her father had left her. She says, "You've got to visualize where you're headed and be very clear about it. Take a polaroid picture of where you're going to be in a few years. Having a mental snapshot of where you are, where you are going, and what you are moving toward is incredibly powerful." Sara also has an amazing work ethic. When her Spanx first got into department stores, she didn't just sit back and see what would happen. She marched into each of the stores and talked to customers and salesclerks herself to convince them to try Spanx. She did this for two whole years to ensure that the brand took off.

Michael Jordan is known as one of the hardest working athletes in the NBA. He also talks about *always* visualizing a free throw before he takes the shot. He also uses visualization to motivate himself. See, he hadn't made his high school basketball team the first time he tried out and he was totally bummed. But he started practicing harder and visualizing his name on the varsity list. He uses that image even today. "Every time I feel tired while exercising and training, I close my eyes to see that picture, to see that list with my name. This usually motivates me to work again."

---

6   https://soar.suny.edu/bitstream/handle/20.500.12648/6523/pes_the-ses/3/fulltext%20%281%29.pdf?sequence=1&isAllowed=y

The same was true for me. Remember when I wrote my manifesto in 2018 and I had no clue how I was going to do it? I had no idea how I would ever be able to speak in front of 500 people, let alone thousands. But I'm a positive energy person and I wanted to really make a positive impact on others' lives. So, I went ahead and wrote my manifesto and said it out loud everyday twice a day. Then I just started visualizing myself being on stage. I visualized myself driving to the airport, being on the plane, and arriving at some big speaking engagement. I visualized myself looking out at the audience and they were all listening really intently. I visualized people coming up afterwards and telling me how helpful what I'd said had been for them. I kept visualizing this in as much detail as I could—what I was wearing, how the room and the stage looked, the sounds, the colors, even the smells.

And you know what? Recently I spoke in front of 4,500 people at one conference and over 6,000 at a different conference, all within a two week timeframe. It took me four years to get there, but within four years, I was speaking on stages with Tony Robbins, Grant and Elena Cardone, Tom Bilyeu, Ryan Serhant, Gary Vaynerchuk, Russell Brunson, and Trent Sheldon—these are huge names and people that, four years before, I couldn't even imagine being associated with! I put my vision out in the Universe, thought about it and visualized it every single day, all long before I had a clue of how to get there.

A friend texted me about two months before I was going to be speaking on stage with Tony Robbins. She and I had gone to a Tony Robbins' event where we did the fire walk a few years before. She reminded me that I had turned to her back then and said, "I'm going to be on stage one day with Tony Robbins." I don't remember saying that to her. I was just starting to get into coaching at that time. She said, "You said you were going to be on stage with Tony Robbins. And now you are!" I still don't remember that I said that but obviously my brain did—and it took me seriously! I worked really hard but I know that building that certainty in my dream was what kept me from giving up along the way.

One of my goals was to speak at Funnel Hacking Live. I went out and bought these gorgeous shiny rhinestone shoes to wear on stage. I called my husband and said, "Babe I just bought my shoes that I'm going to wear at FHL." He said, "Great, love, but you aren't speaking at FHL." I said, "I'm not speaking *yet*, but I will be." So, I bought the shoes, visualized myself on stage wearing them and the next day, Russell Brunson the owner and founder of Click Funnels called me personally and asked me to be a speaker at FHL. It was surreal!!

If you're going to get the results that you want and keep getting results, if you want to build a career, relationships, health and a life that you are in love with, it's going to require repetition so that your vision of success is in your nervous system and it becomes a part of your subconscious. You can't just dabble in this and *try* it a couple of times. You have to master it and make it part of your regular routine so that this vision and certainty gets deeply embedded into every cell.

Visualization Tools

There are thousands of tools to help you visualize your success. One I've always liked is to create a vision board. This isn't for everybody, but visuals often help. I get a poster board and find pictures in magazines of what I'm going after. I might find a couple walking on a beach and write "Fiji, November, 20XX" on it. Or I could use a picture of a big audience and write, "Three speaking engagements for 1000+ people in 20XX." Whenever I look at my vision boards, I stop and imagine how great it feels to have accomplished these things.

A friend of mine was trying to get back in shape. She had a photo album of a fun trip she had taken to Africa several years before and remembered that trip as a time when she felt strong and flexible. So, every morning, she'd pull out that album and look at all the pictures, remembering how she looked and feeling the way it felt. She made sure that she actually felt it in her body and emotions. It made her feel good and inspired her to do what she knew she needed to do to get back into that kind of shape again.

Another way to visualize your success is to just imagine it. When you're stuck at a traffic light or standing in line at the store, rather than grabbing your cell phone or reading The National Enquirer, just get a scene in your head of the success you want for yourself. Get as clear and detailed as you can as you imagine how great it feels, the sights and sounds of it. Put yourself right in the picture. Feel it in your body and in your emotions.

One great way visualization can train your brain is to remember past successes. People tend to remember the bad stuff that happens but what about the great stuff? Remember times when you felt proud of yourself or when you felt really appreciated or loved. Remember times when you overcame a challenge or accomplished something that was hard for you. Remember times when you felt free and really happy. As you remember these good times, take the time to actually relive them, to feel just like you felt then. Pick a few of these great memories so you can pull them out to give you an extra boost when you need it.

I also have my students visualize the day ahead of them, completing everything they set out to do and how good that feels. This is also a great way to "pre-pave" a good outcome for anything that you're facing. For example, if you're going into a meeting that might be difficult or confrontational, rather than worrying about it, Stop, Snap and See. Visualize that meeting the way you would like it to go. Imagine yourself being confident and others being receptive. Imagine an outcome that is positive and maybe even better than you thought possible. When you do this, you're training your brain to find a way for those positive outcomes to happen.

Affirmations

There's a story about Napoleon Hill. Before he wrote *Think and Grow Rich*, Andrew Carnegie challenged him to not only write the book but to do a daily exercise. Mr. Carnegie told Napoleon Hill to stand in front of a mirror 3 times a day and say, "Andrew Carnegie, I'm not only going to match your achievements in life; I'm going to meet you at the post and pass you at the grandstand." Of course, when Napoleon Hill started doing it, he felt pretty silly and didn't really believe that he'd ever be as great as Andrew Carnegie. But he kept at it and after about 3 weeks, he was just walking down the street one day and a thought popped into his head. "Well, it *could* happen." By doing his mirror practice every day, he had pruned away the synapses of his old disbelieving neuropathways and built new ones that were at least open to the possibility of success.

All the highly successful people I've ever heard about talk about not only how hard they work, but also that they had a vision and used visualization and affirmations to achieve their goals. Before Jim Carrey made it in Hollywood, he had to overcome things like dyslexia and a rough childhood. He quit school to work as a janitor and a security guard to help support his family. He bombed in his first attempts at stand-up comedy. He went through disappointment after disappointment but kept telling himself, "Everyone wants to work with me. I'm a really good actor. I have all kinds of great movie offers." Still a relatively unknown actor just barely making ends meet in 1990, he decided to write himself a check for $10MM for "acting services rendered." He put a date of 1995 on it and kept it in his wallet. By 1995, he had been paid exactly $10MM for the movie *Dumb and Dumber.*

Lady Gaga (whose real name is Stefani Germanotta) didn't have an easy start in life. She was bullied as a kid and sexually abused in her teens. Still, she started visualizing and affirming a better life for herself. She used to have her own mantra that she said over and over, "Music is my life, music is my life. The fame is inside of me, I'm going to make a number one record with number one hits." She's now worth over $300 million and is the first person to win an Academy Award, a Grammy, a BAFTA, and a Golden Globe Award in the same year. Is she talented? Heck, yeah. *And* she worked very hard to get to where she is. She studied classical piano, music theory and music history. She wrote songs for other people and played small gigs before she was ever famous. Her affirmative mantra kept her going.

I write this affirmation down each night before I go to bed (most nights). "I Krista Mashore will speak in front of 10,000 of my own people in a motivational transformational speaking event, by 3-21-2025 (that's Steve's birthday!). This is what I think I want. However, I am open to something even better even sooner. Jehovah God, please put me in front of the people and things I need to make this happen. Please make me the best that I can be today and put me in front of the people I need to meet." David Asarnow, someone I hired to help make my company more efficient, taught me this.

I use affirmations all the time because I really believe the affirmations are our thoughts and our thoughts become our things. I'd used them for a while. It really started for me several years ago when I was at the gym and I was having a lot of negative self-talk in my head. I don't even know what was really bothering me, but I knew it wasn't doing me any good. So, I did some research on Google and found people saying, "Listen to this affirmation for six weeks straight and you'll have more success, wealth, health, and abundance."

So, I started doing that, but I took it one step further and I wrote out all the affirmations. I took the affirmations I'd written and recorded them in my own voice. Then I listened to the recording in my own voice every morning for 90 days. I'd just listen to it all the time, before I went to bed (my hubby had to listen to them too lol), on my way to work, while I was cooking breakfast. I'd hear the recording of my positive affirmations then I would repeat them out loud.

By doing the Stop, Snap and Switch process, you're already using a type of affirmation. You're taking some negative thought you've said to yourself and switching it to a more empowering thought. That's a great start.

The type of affirmation that I'm talking about here (and that I did for those 90 days) is to help propel you to your next level. It's when you take your dream or goal and affirm it as already true, already happening. It's in the present tense, like Jim Carrey's "I have all kinds of great movie offers" or Lady Gaga's "I have fame inside of me." It needs to be something that reflects a life that inspires you, like your manifesto.

One of the keys to affirmations is that you say them with *emotion*. Just repeating mindless words over and over won't do anything to create new beliefs. It's only through emotion and feeling that they start creating new neuropathways. So be sure to get your whole body into your affirmations and say them with conviction.

I really suggest that you record them in your own voice. Record them on your phone so you can whip them out and listen to them often. To have any kind of impact on the neuropathways of your brain, you have to repeat your affirmations often. Just saying them once or twice won't cut it. Remember that it took Napoleon Hill 3 whole weeks of repeating his affirmation 3 times daily before his brain kicked in and decided that the affirmation was even a possibility. I tell my students that they need to read their manifestos out loud once in the morning and once at night.

You can also come up with shorter affirmations to inspire you throughout the day, like "I always find a way" or "I am perfectly positioned for massive success." Put these on sticky notes on your computer so you see them when you're working. Put them all over your bathroom mirrors to remind you while you brush your teeth.

Gratitude

"Be thankful for what you have, you'll end up having more. If you concentrate on what you don't have, you will never ever have enough." — *Oprah Winfrey*

One of the most important tools I teach my students is gratitude. When I tell them that gratitude will do more to make them successful than any digital marketing technique I can teach them, they're a little skeptical. But when they actually get into the habit of gratitude, they're amazed by the results they get. "Wait a minute, Krista. How can gratitude get me where I want to go? Don't I have to feel hungry and dissatisfied so I'll stay motivated to get what I want?" Yes and no. Hunger for something is good. But at the same time, you need to train your brain to notice everything that's good and everything that's working in your life. Why? Because then it will want to find more of it. Energy goes where focus flows.

When you express gratitude, your brain releases dopamine and serotonin which make you feel good and positive about life. You know this from your own experience, right? Stop right now and think about something or someone you're really grateful for. Maybe it's your health or your spouse or your dog. Really think about *why* you're grateful for whatever it is. Let yourself think about it and feel that gratitude for a minute or two. Don't you feel better and more positive than you did before?

The optimistic attitude that gratitude builds in you attracts success and gets our brains to notice more opportunities rather than focusing on obstacles. That kind of positive mindset is what we need to achieve what we want. Feeling grateful may not feel effortless at first, yet it's something we can learn to feel most of the time. But a consistent mindset of gratitude won't just happen by feeling grateful for a few minutes every year right before we dig into Thanksgiving turkey! We need to experience gratitude *daily* so that the neuropathways of gratitude get strong and become our more natural mindset.

Research has shown that the practice of gratitude can be powerful in all kinds of ways. We all know (or should know!) that appreciation makes a huge difference in the workplace. In a study run by the Wharton School at the University of Pennsylvania, researchers divided their university fundraisers into 2 random groups. The first group just made phone calls to get donations the same way they always did. The second group had a meeting before getting on the phones where the director of annual giving told them how grateful she was for their hard work. That week, the university fundraisers who were thanked for their efforts made 50% more fund-raising calls than those who weren't thanked.

So, gratitude motivates those who are thanked but what about people *expressing* gratitude? A recent article from the Harvard Medical School stated, "gratitude is strongly and consistently associated with greater happiness. Gratitude helps people feel more positive emotions, relish good experiences, improve their health, deal with adversity, and build strong relationships."

Dr. Robert A. Emmons and Dr. Michael E. McCullough did a study where they divided people up into 3 random groups and asked them to write a few sentences every week. The first group wrote about anything they were grateful for that week. The next group wrote about things that had irritated them or problems they'd run into. The last group just wrote about anything that happened during the week, good or bad.

After 10 weeks, the people who wrote about what they were grateful for reported feeling more optimistic and positive about their lives than the other groups. What was interesting was that they also had *fewer visits to their doctors* than the people who had written about things that upset them!

It's true that gratitude can have a big impact on your health. Dr. Glenn Fox who specializes in the science of gratitude at USC Marshall School of Business said in an interview, "Benefits associated with gratitude include better sleep, more exercise, reduced symptoms of physical pain, lower levels of inflammation, lower blood pressure and a host of other things we associate with better health. The limits to gratitude's health benefits are really in how much you pay attention to feeling and practicing gratitude."

Gratitude can even impact our food choices! A study from the Positive Activities and Well-Being (PAW) Laboratory at the University of California Riverside divided high school students into two groups. All of the students had set a healthy eating goal for themselves, and they were all told to write weekly letters. But one group was asked to write letters of gratitude while the other was told to just list their daily activities. Guess what? The students in the gratitude group significantly improved their eating habits over the ones who didn't.

So, when I tell you that a steady practice of gratitude will literally change your life, I am not exaggerating! Gratitude is one of the major food groups that the Good Wolf thrives on, so you want to feed it daily.

One of the things that I've learned about gratitude is that, even if you're having a horrible day, it's really hard to be angry or cranky or sad when you're being grateful. Whenever you experience gratitude, your brain releases a cocktail of dopamine, oxytocin, and endorphins, the hormones that make you feel happy and loving. And no matter what's going on in your life, we all have things we can be grateful for. As Brene Brown said, *"I don't have to chase extraordinary moments to find happiness. It's right in front of me if I'm paying attention and practicing gratitude."*

When you're practicing being grateful, it's important to really get into the feeling of it. Don't just write a list of things like "I love my daughter." Get into why you love your daughter, what she brings to your life. It might be something like, "I am really grateful that my daughter is going to move back here so that she's close. I'm grateful that we'll get to do mother/daughter things together. I'm grateful that she has decided to take over my real estate business." (Although I didn't anticipate how hard it would be to teach your own kid! OMG she can be so challenging!) Be specific. I often tell my students to choose something that happened in the past 24 hours that they can really, truly feel grateful for. Rather than focusing on what didn't go well, focus on what's working.

A friend was telling me that in her gratitude practice what started coming up for her were things in her past that didn't look positive at the time. "I thought about a boyfriend who had dumped me. It had really hurt at the time but when I saw him years later, he had grown cynical and grouchy and lived a lifestyle that I definitely would not want. I realized that I had dodged a bullet and felt this huge sense of gratitude for that." Today, when I think of some of the challenges in my past, I feel really, truly grateful for them because they caused me to grow and become who I am.

You want to build up a *daily habit* of thinking about everything you're grateful for so that it becomes your default mindset. I teach my students to start the day with gratitude every morning, to jump out of bed and instantly yell something they're grateful for the second their feet hit the floor. Then to sit down and write a list of things they're grateful for. To get the most benefit out of gratitude, you can just write down a few things you're grateful for, big or small, and why you're grateful for them. Then take a few moments to really *feel* the appreciation and good feelings you have about whatever you wrote down. It's great to feel grateful for people and things in your life right now. It's also good to feel grateful for things in your past and *grateful in advance for things in your future!*

Another way to strengthen your gratitude muscle is to *express* gratitude frequently. You can schedule in a weekly gratitude time to write a few thank you notes. You can also set a goal of 5 texts or phone calls per week to people you appreciate. My friend Chas did this and sent a text to his mentor who he loved so much to express how grateful he was and what an impact he had made on his life. The next day, his mentor passed away. When he told that story, it was so powerful that he had a roomful of us crying!

One thing I've learned is that being specific when you express gratitude makes it more powerful for both you and the person receiving it. For example, rather than just "Thanks for all your hard work," take the time to point out exactly what you appreciate. "I really appreciate that you are so accountable and whenever I ask you to do something, I can trust that it will get done." Or how about when you receive a gift? "Every time I wear this sweater, it will put me in a good mood because

I'll think of you and how fun you are!" Much more powerful than just "thank you," right?

Gratitude is also a perfect tool for your Stop, Snap, and Be Grateful. When you catch yourself thinking negatively or complaining, just stop, snap your wristband and switch to thinking about something you're grateful for. A good dose of gratitude is a great antidote for any kind of toxic thought you're having. And if everything seems to be going down the tubes? That's when you need to feel and express a truckload of gratitude!

People look at me like I'm crazy when I say this. At the time I'm writing this, the market is tanking, interest rates are rising, inflation is going crazy, there's a major war overseas—yikes! And now Monkeypox is taking over! What the heck is Monkeypox?!? It's really easy to get caught up in what's *not* working. But no matter what's going on, we've all got a lot that we can be grateful for.

Even if you're struggling financially right now, odds are you are doing better than 97% of the world's population. And, more importantly, you have the opportunity to turn your financial problems around. Be grateful!

Mortgage rates may have priced you out of the market, but if you have a roof over your head, you are more fortunate than over 1.6 billion people in the world who don't have decent shelter or have no shelter at all. Be grateful.

Even if the prices of your favorite foods have skyrocketed, you're still more fortunate than nearly 50 million Americans (including about 16 million children) who can't afford to put *any* food on the table on a regular basis. Be grateful.

If you have food in your refrigerator, clothes on your back, a roof over your head, and a place to sleep, you're richer than 77% of this world. Be grateful. Learning to have the attitude of gratitude will improve your life in so many ways. It will also be key to achieving what you want whether it's more business success, improved health or better relationships.

"If you make your prayers an expression of gratitude and thanksgiving for the blessings you already have, instead of requests for things you do not have, you will obtain results much faster." —Napoleon Hill

Celebration

"The way to measure your progress is backward against where you started, not against your ideal." —Dan Sullivan

Almost everyone celebrates when they reach a big goal, right? They'll pop the champagne open after landing a big deal. They'll do a crazy end zone dance when they score a touchdown. They'll reward themselves with a new outfit after achieving a weight goal. But if you want to maintain motivation, you have to celebrate all the small victories, the tiny accomplishments and improvements along the way. Why? As I always tell my students, "What gets celebrated, gets replicated!" And small successes and accomplishments turn into *massive results* over time.

I read a book by Dan Sullivan and Dr. Benjamin Hardy called *The Gap And The Gain*. In it, the authors explain that when you're going towards a goal, there's the gap and then there's the gain. The gap is everything between where you are now and where you want to be. We all tend to focus on the gap and what's across that gap and the fact that we *aren't* there yet.

We hardly even pay attention to the *gain* and the fact that we're closing the gap and getting closer. We barely notice how far we've come or how much we've accomplished as we work toward what we want. We may not be our ideal self yet and may not have reached our goal, but we *have* taken steps and made some gains. Yes, we do want to focus on where we want to go and keep our eyes on the prize. But at the same time, it's important to enjoy the journey and acknowledge everything that you're doing right and how you're progressing and all the wins you've had along the way.

The reason you want to acknowledge and celebrate all the small wins is that every gain you make is a success and *success builds confidence*. If you don't focus on your daily wins, you're wasting an opportunity to train your brain toward confidence and success. You want your brain to notice those daily challenges you successfully overcame so that when the next issue comes up, it says, "No problem. We got this." You want to acknowledge all those good ideas you implemented each day or times you stepped out of your comfort zone so that your brain knows, "Yep, that's what we do, and it feels good when do those things." If you just ignore your daily progress, you're not strengthening that neuropathway as powerfully as when you give yourself a big high five for the steps you're taking.

I know that sometimes when you're in the middle of the journey, it's hard to notice how you're improving because the improvements seem so *small*. When you get to where you're trying to go, it's easy to forget where you started, and you certainly don't remember all the steps you took along the way. That's why I teach my students to take notice of what they did well and what worked for them literally every single day. It doesn't have to be earth shattering. Just any small improvement or good effort they made. Then I tell them to focus on what they're going to do well tomorrow and what's going to work for them tomorrow. Remember that your brain has been wired to help you get whatever you focus on. Your thoughts, your focus, your values, and your beliefs all turn into your actions. Then your habits and your actions create your outcomes. So, you want your mindset to be targeted toward successful outcomes.

I am learning every day to allow the space between where I am and where I want to be to inspire me and not terrify me. —Tracee Ellis Ross

We've got to start training our brain and cultivating a mindset that looks at all of the good stuff happening right now. When you constantly look at what you're *not* doing well, what didn't work, what went wrong, what you didn't accomplish, you're basically telling the brain to keep on doing more of *that*. The more that we recognize the gains and the small wins and focus on what we're doing well, the more that the brain realizes, "Okay, you did that well and it felt good with all that dopamine releasing. Let's go ahead and let's figure out how to get more of that."

How to celebrate? The first thing I teach my students to do is to write down everything they did well that day and any wins, big or small. Just by acknowledging those positive steps on a daily basis, you're beginning to strengthen those neuropathways. Then give yourself a pat on the back for what you did right. Give yourself an "attaboy" or "attagirl" like you would give to someone on your team. Give yourself a high five! Stop, Snap, and Celebrate yourself all through the day! Do this every night right before you go to bed so that, rather than worrying about all you *didn't* accomplish or thinking about what you *don't* have yet, you go to sleep with the good feeling of a successful day. My dad always told me, "Success breeds success" and the more we recognize our small wins and successes the more our brains will be wired to get us more of them. We literally train our brains to get us what we want!

Another way to acknowledge your progress is by keeping a journal. When you keep a journal, you can go back and remind yourself where you came from, that your new "normal" was just a dream back then. You can remind yourself that what you had trouble doing back then is easier for you now. And that means that whatever is hard for you today will be easier one day in the future! You can remind yourself of the risks you took or challenges you overcame. And that means whatever challenges you're facing today can be overcome as well! With each memory and celebration of your gains, the neuropathways of success get stronger and stronger. And as we say doing the Hokey Pokey, "That's what it's all about!"

"The more you praise and celebrate your life, the more there is in life to celebrate."
—Oprah Winfrey

Building Momentum

By doing the exercises I've shared with you (and I'm assuming that you've been doing the exercises otherwise you're just wasting your time!), you're starting to build the positive mindset that will get you anywhere you want to go! And I know that you're the type of person who wants to be the best that you can be because you've taken the time to read this book. So now is the time that you need to start *taking action*.

If you've discovered a really compelling *why* for yourself, you're probably feeling all jazzed and eager to leap in. But what about next week when you're feeling tired and not getting results yet? Or what about the first time you screw up or run into a problem and get knocked off kilter? That first flash of enthusiasm isn't enough to keep you going. To stay persistent and take the action you need to take to get where you want to go, you need *momentum.*

Momentum is the difference between success and failure. It's the difference between sustained success and someone who tries for a little while and then falls by the wayside. I've seen so many people come and go over the years and the difference between those people and people who push through, who never give up and who keep going is that *they understand and use momentum.*

When people say to me, "You know, I *tried* that, it didn't work", I can tell you exactly what they're really saying. They're saying, "I didn't really believe this was going to work so I didn't give it my all. I was afraid I wouldn't succeed so I backed off." If you're just *trying*, you don't have momentum.

As Yoda says, "Do. Or do not. There is no try."

> When people say to me, "You know, I tried that, it didn't work", I can tell you exactly what they're really saying. They're saying, "I didn't really believe this was going to work so I didn't give it my all. I was afraid I wouldn't succeed so I backed off."

Momentum is built on two things: 1) Your compelling why, that fire in your belly that drives you to keep going, and 2) your sense of *certainty* and belief that you can achieve your goal. As you're going for your dream, those are the two things that we have to make bullet-proof. How? By visualizing yourself successfully getting positive results in advance which creates more certainty, and by reminding yourself of your compelling why *every single day* to light that fire in your belly. When you do this, your goal and vision become like an obsession. You wake up every morning thinking about it and eager to take action. Everywhere you look, you see opportunities and possibilities of how to get where you want to go. When you hit a roadblock, you don't worry it to death, but you blast through it and don't let it stop you.

Remember Tony Robbins' Success Cycle?

THE SUCCESS CYCLE

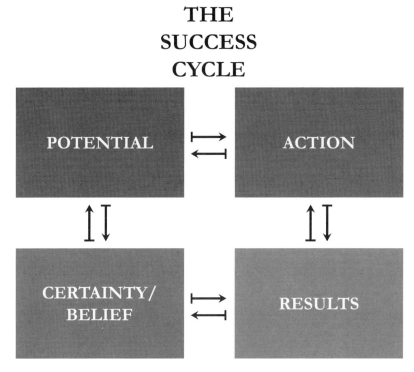

When you've got your compelling why figured out, you need to make sure that your certainty and belief is super strong. With that, you'll tap into your potential so that when you act, you act with confidence, creativity, and high energy. And when you act with confidence, creativity, and high energy, you get positive results. When you get positive results, that builds your certainty and belief, and the cycle keeps going. At every step of the way, you feel excited knowing that you're heading in the right direction and highly motivated to keep going until you reach your ultimate goal.

But if you don't build up that certainty first, if you're unsure of yourself or you doubt that your strategy will work, you just won't tap into your full potential. Rather than taking massive, ferocious action, you'll hedge your bets and hesitate. You'll hold back and run back to your comfort zone. And what happens with that kind of action? Frankly, not much, except that you reinforce your belief that "I don't have what it takes" or "This doesn't really work." And that de-motivating cycle repeats itself too: Your poor results make you feel less certain, so you tap even less of your potential and take even weaker action and get even worse results!

Momentum works both ways. It can be positive or negative and sometimes you get stuck in the negative momentum cycle. You can't get yourself to take the action you know you need to take. Why? Either you've disconnected from your why or you've lost your certainty that you can achieve what you want. You've started listening again to the Bad Wolf rather than the Good Wolf that you've been feeding.

One thing successful people have in common is they've developed the *skill of momentum*. They weren't born with it, but they learned it and are really good at using it when they find themselves slipping into a negative momentum cycle. They know exactly what they need to do: Reconnect to their compelling why and vision and strengthen their certainty that they can achieve what they've set out to do. You can learn to use this skill too, by visualizing success in your mind in advance and constantly reconnecting to your vision and your why. You've got to keep that fire lit in your belly and you've got to rewire your neuropathways so that your sense of certainty runs automatically through your whole body.

Building Your Limitless Abundance Foundation: The Daily Sheet

We all know about eating a good breakfast, right? Well, eating a good "brain breakfast" is even more important! And honestly, folks, turning on the news first thing in the morning is NOT going to be a positive start! So, what else can you do? The bottom line is to start your day doing whatever makes you feel good, energized and positive, *and* to set yourself up for having *unstoppable momentum* for the day by visualizing your successful results in advance.

I have a personal morning ritual that I teach all my students: I get up and exercise and dress first (even if you're working from home, getting dressed is still a good idea). Then I sit down and visualize the life I want to live, and I visualize my current goals, experiencing them as if they're already a done deal. I visualize them vividly and I let myself feel all the awesome feelings of having accomplished what I set out to do.

This may still seem too woo-woo for you or Pollyanna-ish. But it's not. It's science. So, you can choose to believe me (and science) or you can stick to your old beliefs about it. But ask yourself first: Which belief will serve you better?

Next, I read my manifesto. Again, I really get into the experience of what is important about it and connect emotionally again with my compelling why, so it's not just a thought but I can feel it in my body. And finally, I fill out my Daily Sheet. Part of it gets filled out in the morning and the rest is filled out at night:

66 99

FOCUS/QUOTE OF THE DAY

☐ Visualize my day ☐ Attend Skin in the Game ☐ Wrote out 6 activities

☐ Read manifesto ☐ Showed gratitude ☐ Pay it forward

Evening Rituals

☐ Show Gratitude

☐ Calendar out my day for tomorrow

☐ Give myself permission to dream of what I need

☐ Visualize my day for tomorrow

Today's Hit List & Time Blocks (Hard stuff first!)

HOURS

1._____ ____

2._____ ____

3._____ ____

4._____ ____

5._____ ____

6._____ ____

☐ I blocked out the time in my calendar!

☐ I am committed to the "Touch It Once" Rule

I Am Grateful For...

1._____

_____

2._____

_____

3._____

_____

Today's Gains

1._____

_____

2._____

_____

3._____

_____

Predicting Tomorrow's Gains

1._____

_____

2._____

_____

3._____

_____

P1 ☐☐ ☐☐ P2 ☐☐ ☐☐ P3 ☐☐ ☐☐ P4 ☐☐ ☐☐

The Daily Sheet really sets me up for the day. It includes all of the success habits I've learned over the years. I do it before the day gets away with me because I know from experience these habits are critical to my continued success. It has a Hit List of things I'll do during the day as well as lines to fill in.

I like to start my Daily Sheet with either an affirmative statement of something I'm working on (like, *"I am a patient listener who really seeks to understand others"* or *"I have plenty of time in my day to do what needs to get done"*) or an inspirational quote. I really like learning and getting motivated by someone else's wise words. Sometimes, I'll use the same quote for several days in a row. I have so many of these that sometimes it's hard to choose and other times, a quote will jump out at me as being absolutely what I need for that day. Here are a few I like:

"Find out who you are and be that person. That's what your soul was put on this Earth to be. Find that truth, live that truth and everything else will come."
— *Ellen DeGeneres*
"Turn your wounds into wisdom."
— *Oprah Winfrey*
"It's never too late to be who you might have been."
— *George Eliot*
"It's better to have loved and lost than never to have loved at all."
—*Alfred Lord Tennyson.*

I love this last one because it's about taking risks and action. Even if you take action and fail, it's better to have tried than not to have tried at all because you'll learn and improve as you go!

I also love a quote from my dad who is one of my most loved, respected and favorite people in the world: *"A marriage is made up of two loving, forgiving, compromising people."* That quote has literally helped make my marriage what it is today!! Thank you, Dad, I love you dearly!!!

Then I write down four to six things I'm grateful for. I spend a moment to really *feel* grateful, not just throw some words on the paper. The "attitude of gratitude" is one of the most powerful mindsets you can have! When you feel and show gratitude, you get more of what you're grateful for. Energy goes where focus flows. So, being grateful for all the blessings in your life really helps to set your day up right.

From the night before, I've already written out six things I'm going to accomplish for the day. This isn't a To Do list because I really think

To Do lists are counterproductive. It seems like I can never get every-thing done on a To Do list, so it makes me feel deflated at the end of the day. Now I do a "Hit List." These are the absolutely most import-ant things I need to accomplish in a day. I take those 6 things and time block them into my day (I'll talk about time blocking in a later section of the book), always tackling the hardest ones first.

Then in the morning, I look at this Hit List and the time blocks and pre-pave success for the day by visualizing the successful outcome of each task or interaction. For example, if I've got a meeting coming up, I visualize how I want the meeting to go, what we'll get accomplished, and how great my team is working together and coming up with awe-some ideas.

Either that night or during the day, I write down all of my wins for the day, like things I accomplished and challenges I faced. At night, right before I go to sleep, I think about the day's wins and let my-self feel great about them. I also write out my top of mind goal. For example, as I'm writing this book, what I write at night is "I, Krista Mashore, will speak in front of 10,000 of my own people in a moti-vational transformational speaking event, by 3-21-2025 (that's Steve's birthday!). This is what I think I want. However, I am open to some-thing even better even sooner. Please put me in front of the people and things I need to make this happen. Please make me the best that I can be today and put me in front of the people I need to meet."

When you combine the Daily Sheet with using Stop, Snap, and Switch and your affirmations throughout the day, it's like an insurance policy. No matter what happens, you'll have a more positive mindset and you'll be much more able to handle whatever life throws at you. You'll stay on track for what's truly important to you. You'll feel more confident and happier, and you'll have the momentum to take the ac-tion you need to take to get where you want to go.

Execution and implementation, taking action is the ultimate power. Taking action trumps knowledge every day of the week. So next we'll talk about how to make sure you're taking *effective action*.

Taking Effective Action

"The most difficult thing is the decision to act, the rest is merely tenacity. The fears are paper tigers. You can do anything you decide to do. You can act to change and control your life..."
—Amelia Earhart

No matter what you're going after, you'll need to take action to get there, right? Say, you want to find a life partner and start a family. You have a strong why and you've put together a vision of what that relationship and that family looks like. You've worked on your mindset and you're feeling positive about it. Awesome! But now you can't just sit at home watching romantic comedies waiting for Mr. or Ms. Right to show up on your doorstep! You need to get up off the couch and take action! As Ann Landers used to say, *"Opportunities are usually disguised as hard work, so most people don't recognize them."* (If you want to know why action is so important, go to KristaMashore.com/SSSBook and check out this video: Creating the Momentum You Need)

I love reading some of W. Clement Stone's books. He lived from 1902 to 2002 and was a businessman and one of the wealthiest men of his time. He believed that *delay is the enemy of wealth*. In fact, he would say "Do it now!" 100 times each day and he made his staff do the same. You need to take action now, starting where you are and what you have and allow yourself to be imperfect. I always tell my students, "When you feel worried, or tired, or like you can't handle something, just say 'Do it now!' When you feel overwhelmed, just say, 'Do it now!'" The enemy in your thoughts, the one holding you back is keeping you from greatness. When you hear the enemy in your thoughts come in, just say, "Do it now!" Even better, do it now with the *certainty* that you'll succeed!

To get positive results, you can't just take any old action. It doesn't matter how positive you are, if you take the *wrong* action or *ineffective* actions, you won't get the results you want. You'll just spin your wheels and stay exactly where you are—only now you'll be exhausted and discouraged. So many people tell me that they're working hard to achieve their goals but a lot of what they're doing is busy-ness (meaningless busy work) that won't get them very far. You need to take *effective action* to get where you want to go.

Whenever you are creating something new in your life, you can do it the *hard way* or the *easier way*. The hard way is the way most people approach it. They don't really know what they want, and they don't set definite goals. They don't visualize and rehearse their success in advance to engage their reticular activating system (RAS) working for them, so they don't notice opportunities. They get distracted by shiny objects along the way and wander off onto paths that aren't heading in the direction they need to be heading.

And probably worst of all, they try to figure out how to do it all by themselves! They ignore the wisdom and experience of those who've succeeded before them. It's like they've got a machete and they're hacking their way through a dense jungle all by themselves—when there's a nice, clear path that's going to the exact same place! Hacking through the jungle is not only hard, it also takes a long, *long* time.

Then there's the easier way. The easier way starts by knowing exactly what you want and having that fire in your belly to get there. The easier way involves rehearsing your success in advance over and over in your mind until your RAS wakes up and says, "Whoa! She's *serious* about this! We better look for things that would help her!" The easier way means having a laser focus on your goals so that distractions become irritating, not interesting. The easier way means *modeling* the people who have succeeded before you, not reinventing the wheel. And when you do this, it's not only easier, it's a much, *much* shorter journey. You can literally knock years off the time it takes to succeed.

Coaches and Mentors

Modeling someone who has achieved what you want to achieve is the key to speeding up getting the results you want. When I talk about modeling, I mean not only learning to *do what they do* but learning *to think like they think.* If someone has spent twenty years of their life figuring something out, making mistakes and finding solutions, reading and studying hundreds of books, and spending hundreds of thousands of dollars to tap the best coaches, consultants, and mentors, why would you want to spend time and energy building that same foundation yourself?!? Wouldn't you rather *start* with what they know and build on it? Instead of wasting your time and energy, you can model those successful people and extract the knowledge that took them 20 years of trial and error to get. They can teach you the principles and strategies that work *and* help you avoid wasting time and money on strategies that don't work.

I've had a number of coaches and mentors throughout my career, and I've got to tell you that I don't know where I'd be without them! In fact, I still have coaches and mentors to this day. Early on, one of them was within the real estate industry and some were in the training industry. Most were from different types of businesses. But all of them have had the type of success I want to have. They've all been very open and sincere about sharing their expertise and experience with me. They're all authentic and the kind of person that I really want to emulate, not just in business but in their personal lives. That's important because to me, true success isn't just making a lot of money, or buying the fancy car and big home, or finding Mr. or Ms. Right. The success I want—and that I want for all of us—means happiness and fulfillment in *all* areas of life.

You may think I'm crazy for spending so much money, and 23 years ago, I would have agreed with you. But hiring these professionals who have walked the path I want to walk is the reason that my success came so quickly. I've collapsed timeframes and taken a quantum leap by doing what they did well and avoiding what they didn't do right. Modeling and mimicking them is how I'm creeping up on my 3rd multi-million dollar-a-year business now.

Of course, not all mentors and "coaches" are great. Here are some questions that will help you decide whether a certain person is right for you.

Do they really have the success you want? A lot of people out there teach courses or claim to be coaches, but they haven't really achieved success themselves. They're more interested in teaching about success than succeeding themselves. It's like that old saying, "Those who can, do. Those who can't, teach." That's not true of all teachers but don't learn from someone who wasn't successful and then tries to teach how to do the thing they themselves couldn't do!

Other coaches have been training or coaching for decades, but they still teach you to do things the way it was done thirty years ago. Make sure the people you're learning from have actually done what they're teaching you to do. For example, if you're wanting to build a business, then they've built a business. If you're wanting to find and create a lasting relationship, then they themselves have the kind of relationship you want.

Are they passionate about what they do? You want a coach or mentor who is passionate about their work, who is constantly learning and trying different approaches. Someone who really knows what they're talking about yet who will admit when they don't know an answer. Choose the person who takes pride in the quality of everything they do, who treats every project like a million-dollar project and every client or mentee like their new best friend.

Are they sincerely offering what you need to know? Sometimes more experienced businesses and professionals want to help, but they're afraid of giving up "the secret sauce." They have some tricks up their sleeves that could really help you out, but they're afraid to share it. Make sure the person you choose as a mentor or coach is generous with what they know. This is why it's often a good idea to use a paid coach. If you're just getting free advice from someone, chances are that they're holding back the secret sauce!

Are they the kind of person you want to be? Maybe you know some hot shot who has made a ton of money and is willing to mentor you, but you sense that they aren't quite ethical in how they operate. Don't even go near that person! You'll end up getting tainted by their reputation as well. What about the workaholic who has no time for herself, her family, or her community? Working hard is one thing, but is that who you want to be? Do you really want a relationship coach who is on her fifth marriage?

Are they willing to hold your feet to the fire? One of the biggest benefits of coaches or mentors is that they hold you accountable. They don't just take your money or spend time spouting advice. They really care that you take what they're teaching you and implement it. They really want you to succeed and they're willing to tell you if you're headed in a wrong direction.

People who want to achieve something big in life need someone to guide them. The number one reason is that we all need *accountability*. We need help. We need support. We're all human. A few years ago, I hired a leadership coach. Why? Because my businesses were getting huge and needed me to be a great leader. I knew that wasn't my strong suit and I wanted it to be. I also found a business-scaling coach because my coaching business was growing at a very fast pace, and I wanted to make sure my clients still got excellent service. I needed these coaches for their knowledge but also to have accountability so that I actually implemented all the things they taught me.

When I was in a training with Tony Robbins, he mentioned that Oprah gets coached by him. Tony once said to her, "Oprah, you're one of the most powerful, richest women in the world. Why are you coaching with me?" She said, "I need accountability." I figure that if Oprah—who is a gazillionaire and one of the most successful people on the planet—needs accountability to keep reaching her goals, we all do!

I've spent hundreds of thousands of dollars on coaches and mentors, and you know what? It's come back to me literally one hundred-fold. They've not only helped me build my businesses, but they've helped me become the person I need to be to be a leader. They've helped me become a better mate, parent, friend, and definitely a better boss/leader. They've taught me success principles and strategies that apply to all areas of life. They're the reason I was inspired to become a coach myself, to pass on all the gifts they gave me to others.

Mastermind

Another way to get that accountability is with a mastermind. My mastermind group has had a huge impact on my success, especially when I was starting up my coaching business. Being part of a mastermind was one of the principles of success Napoleon Hill discovered when he interviewed successful people like Henry Ford, Thomas Edison, Theodore Roosevelt, and John D. Rockefeller. He talks about mastermind groups in his books *The Law of Success* and *Think and Grow Rich*. He described a mastermind as two or more people who come together "in harmony" to solve problems. A mastermind is like a brain trust where like-minded people help one another succeed. People like Warren Buffet, Bill Gates, Oprah, Richard Branson, and Charles Schwab have all used mastermind groups. (Wouldn't you love to be a fly on the wall with *those* groups!)

Masterminds can be about business and career. But they can also focus on spiritual or personal growth or on certain issues like wildlife conservation or parenting. Whatever the focus, masterminds have certain things in common:

You give and receive. When you have a coach or mentor, you get advice, feedback and guidance. In a mastermind group, you not only *get* those things, but you *give* those things to the other people in the group. It's a two-way street and everyone in the group is supposed to participate. When you do this, everyone feels truly invested in each other's success.

Your mastermind partners are focused on the same thing and heading in the same direction. For example, if your mastermind is about raising children, you may not have the exact same goals for your kids. But your basic philosophy about parenting is similar to others in the group. (If it isn't, you'll spend more time arguing than helping each other!) In a business mastermind, you might be in different industries or types of business, but you'll all share similar business philosophies, and you'll all aspire to a similar the level of success in business.

Everyone in a mastermind *sincerely* wants success for the others as well as for themselves. Each person will have a different definition of what success looks like for themselves and different goals.

But it's important that everyone in the group is supportive and doesn't try to force their own idea of success on others. This means you probably don't want to be in a mastermind with your direct competitors!

I've been in one mastermind group where it felt like everyone was using it as a pitch-fest to push their business or service. I quit that one. I've also had someone recommend a business or service just because they heard their pitch in their mastermind, but they hadn't ever worked with them (and it turns out that the person recommended wasn't that great) but they'd heard them pitch and wanted to be supportive because they were in the mastermind together. So be careful of giving or taking that type of recommendation.

A mastermind group is a totally safe place. To be effective, a mastermind has to be a place where people can trust one another and be honest about whatever issues they're facing. Everyone needs to know that the other people have their best interests at heart, even if the feedback they're giving is tough to take at times.

Mastermind groups are *committed* to one another and to their own goals. Part of the magic of a mastermind is that everyone is *committed*. They take their own goals and the goals of others very seriously. They do their best to support one another by sharing connections and resources. When someone gets advice from the group, they'll implement it. When someone gives advice, they really focus to come up with the best ideas they can. And that's one of the huge benefits of a mastermind: People in the group are expected to be accountable and do what they say they're going to do.

For my students, we've set up a tool to help everyone be accountable to their commitments that we call "Skin in the Game." They call into their group every single morning at the same time. Each person sets one personal goal and one business goal per day. So, it might be something like, "I commit to working out for 45 minutes and I commit to working on my sales page letter for 2 hours today." The next day, everyone reports on the commitments they made the day before. If they kept their commitments and accomplished what they said they would, they announce their new commitments for the day. If not, they say what got in their way and how they will change their behavior in the future to make sure they keep their commitment. Then they make up a new commitment. It doesn't have to be the same one. They can modify their commitment, but the objective is to make sure they commit to doing something they can actually do. Can you see how powerful this would be to keep you on track? The students who take advantage of Skin in the Game make 10 times more progress than those who don't!

This works so well because Skin in the Game acts like an anchor to keeping your commitments. You don't want to let your group down and you don't want to have to report back that you didn't do what you said you would. It's also a great start to your day being around like minded people who share common goals about being the best version of themselves both personally and professionally. People swear by it. I've had hundreds of people tell me it's the catalyst to their success. They get more done in a day than a typical week and more in a week than they used to get done in a month. When you stack up each tiny commitment day after day it adds up to massive results and creates positive momentum.

Focus

"Lack of direction, not lack of time, is the problem. We all have twenty-four-hour days." — Zig Ziglar

Did you know that studies have shown that a lot of very successful people have ADHD? Being able to see hundreds of opportunities and potential challenges all at once can be a superpower! That said, one of the biggest keys to achieving what you want is the ability to *focus*. Trying to go after a zillion goals or opportunities all at the same time is crazymaking! Plus, you end up making very little progress if any. But when you zero in on just one to three goals at once and if you focus all of your creativity, energy, and brainpower to the task or project in front of you, it's amazing what you can accomplish!

It's not just concentrating on the goal or task at hand. It's learning *where* to put your focus. Having a more positive mindset helps a lot with this. For example, I no longer focus on what isn't going right, on small irritations, or the obstacles in my path. Instead, I place my focus on what's working, the small steps I'm taking, and visualizing my ultimate success. Energy flows where focus goes, right?

I've learned to focus on what I can change, not what I can't. None of us can change the weather, the economy, or the fact that the person you have a crush on is married to someone else. What you can change is your response to it. *Every* circumstance, no matter how stinky it looks, has an opportunity waiting to be discovered. Put your focus on finding that opportunity.

I've learned to focus on past successes, not past failures. I don't keep putting my screw-ups on instant replay in my mind. Once I've figured out the lessons from something that didn't work, I do my best to forget about it. Focusing on that past failure will only drain your confidence and make you fearful. You don't want to focus on "not screwing up again." You need to focus on succeeding at achieving your goal. We're playing to win, not to "not lose," right?

Another important part of focus has to do with making sure you're productive and effective rather than just "busy." So many people have the best intentions, but they let themselves get scattered. At the end of the day, they can't figure out why the heck they didn't seem to get anything done! They get so caught up with busywork that they never get to the really important actions they could have taken.

Action Versus Distraction

One thing a lot of us have to learn is the difference between *actions* and *distractions*. There's just so much noise out there all the time! Texts, emails, calls, people who want to chat—how much time do they eat up in a day? What about the drama kings and queens who have to tell you their latest catastrophe? I always say, "Don't let someone else's crisis become yours." In reality, it's rarely a crisis anyhow but it drags you down the drama hole. How much value do you get out of that kind of thing compared to the value you'd get from actions you *know* you should be taking instead? We can't always totally ignore distractions, but we can at least schedule them for certain blocks of time in the day. Don't let them encroach on time that you could spend on actions that will make a real impact.

Today, we have so many distractions coming at us. In a Careerbuilder. com survey, they found that distractions from cell phones are most common (52% of the 2,000 people said it was their top distraction), then comes the internet (44%), and social media (36%). A study from Oxford Economics says that general noise is another distraction.

Another study showed that when you're distracted from what you're doing, it takes an average of *23 minutes* to get you back into really focusing on what you were doing again. At first, I found that hard to believe, but I've read numerous studies that agree with this. It's why a lot of people feel like they're always busy but they're never able to get anything done.

I've learned to schedule when I'll handle certain distractions, like responding to phone calls, texts, and emails. My clients and team know that I'll return phone calls between certain hours and respond to emails during certain hours. It's important to set expectations so you don't feel the pressure of someone freaking out because you didn't reply to their email or text within five minutes. If something is time sensitive or urgent, I've got team members who are assigned to respond. Sometimes it's about an issue only I can handle but I try to make this the rare exception.

Sometimes we even create our own distractions! For example, say that your goal is to write a book. Hey, I've been there and done that six times now, so I know it's a big project! My editor taught me that one of the ways new writers get themselves distracted is that they try to make every sentence perfect from the start. They go over and over that first page or chapter and never move on to the next. She says, "You can go back and make it better later. But you'll never get any traction with the book or write the last chapter if you spend all your time rehashing something you've already written." And actually, that applies to everything! If you spin your wheels trying to make your eHarmony profile perfect, or your client presentation perfect, or your first big speech perfect, you'll never get out there and take the next step.

Play Your Position

One aspect of focus is learning to focus on what is *yours* to do, not what others could or should be doing. I've never played football, but

I've heard that football coaches tell their teams all the time to "Play your position." In other words, if the guy next to you is supposed to catch the ball and you're supposed to tackle whoever comes near him, then trust your teammate to do his job and you do yours. If you're constantly doing what others are supposed to be doing, you won't be effective at your own job.

If as a business owner you've turned your marketing over to someone in your organization, let them do it. Train them and critique their work but don't jump in and do the job for them. If you've told your kids that the new puppy is their responsibility, hold them to it. Show them what to do and maybe even remind them, but don't leap in and take over. Let them experience the consequences. (I know, easier said than done, right?) If you've told your assistant that he can take over putting together meeting agendas, let him do it.

To accomplish your goals, it's important to spend your time and energy doing the things that only *you* can do. Of course, sometimes, it almost all falls on you! When I started my first business in real estate, I had to do it all from marketing to contacting vendors to reviewing contracts. When my girls were really little and I was a single mom, everything from bringing home a paycheck to bringing in the laundry, to tucking them in at night and wiping away their tears, was all on me. But as soon as I started making money, I started hiring people to do the things that other people could handle so I could focus on what only *I* could do, like meeting with clients or spending quality time with my daughters.

One Thing at a Time

To really be productive and effective, you need to do *one thing at a time*. Your vision and goal probably have a lot of moving pieces to them and maybe thousands of action steps you need to take to put them all together. It can get totally overwhelming! I remember a period when I was first launching my coaching business and I was doing way too many things all at once. I was getting my website up, overseeing the design of my logo, working to get my first book done, re-doing all the video webinars I had created, and so many other things that I can't even count them! It was crazy! I was working with a bunch of different vendors and experts who all had different priorities for me. I was overwhelmed and stressed out. And I was not getting *anything* done on *any* of it.

I've learned to not let myself get yanked in all directions like that. Now, I focus on one step at a time and do a good job on it before moving to the next. One of my coaches, Russell Brunson, says over and over "Just One Thing!" And, boy, is he right. Once I understood the importance of focusing on just one thing at a time, I started to be much more efficient and productive.

Make sure your focus stays on what you need to do in this moment, not all the pieces of everything you need to do. Studies have shown that if you focus on one thing at a time *exclusively* rather than multitasking, you actually get more done than if you try to multitask. Yes, ladies, this includes us too! Research also shows that the more we multitask the harder it is to stay on task. It's a vicious cycle! We think we can do 3 things at once, but can we really? Can we write a text message or an email while having a conversation and *really* hear what the other person is saying? No, we can't.

Plan Your Action

> *"One of the things I realized is that if you do not take control over your time and your life, other people will gobble it up. If you don't prioritize yourself, you constantly start falling lower and lower on your list…"*
> —*Michelle Obama*

What helps me focus and be effective is, first of all, making sure that I know *exactly* what I need to get done in a day, in each week, and each month. I do this by sitting down and first thinking about my Limitless Abundance Map, the overall vision for what I want. Then I decide which areas I need to focus on. I won't ignore the others, but maybe my first priority is to get my health and my financial life in order. So, I write down one or two goals for the year that will get me closer to achieving abundance in those areas. Then I break that goal down into quarterly goals. What do I need to accomplish in the first quarter? The second, third and fourth quarters? Then because each quarter has 12 weeks, I break it down further and figure out what I need to accomplish each week to attain the quarterly and yearly goal.

Rather than just responding to whatever shows up, I spend time figuring out the main thing I want to accomplish each quarter. What's the biggest, most *important* thing? What's my priority for each quarter? To get there, what do I need to accomplish each week? Finally, at the beginning of each week, I sit down and figure out what steps I need to take every single day to get to my weekly and quarterly goals. (If you'd like to learn more about goal setting, go to KristaMashore.com/ SSSBook and check out the Goal Setting Training video I did on it)

Your quarterly action plan may change if you learn something new or come upon a new opportunity. In fact, every so often, you really should evaluate whether your overall strategy to reach your goal is working. If you're on the wrong track, you need to find a different way. But changing your plan every three days will just keep you swimming in circles. Too many people give up on their action plan before it has a chance to show them results! Stick to your first action plan and really work it. Stay with it long enough to give it a chance. Then if it's not getting results, find a new strategy and create an action plan based on the new strategy.

When you're just beginning to take steps toward a big goal, and especially when you're just starting to put the basics in place, you can feel like you aren't getting anywhere. By writing down your yearly goal, your quarterly priorities, and what you must accomplish every week and every day, you can make sure that the important things get done. It also lets you track your progress and see that you're on your way. You may not be at the finish line, but you can still celebrate the important steps you're taking to get there.

Remember tracking your progress is essential. What you track grows and you have a reference to evaluate your progress. I recommend trying to get an 80% completion score on average on the action steps you're taking. If you get a 65% to 85% score on your progress, you're on the right track. We don't have to have 100%. We just need to shoot for a B- and everyone can get a B- if you put in the effort! That will get you the results you want and if you do this consistently, you'll be amazed at how far you go and how quickly you can get there. Thinking we can do 100% all of the time is setting ourselves up for failure. Trying to get 100% all the time isn't reasonable and you'll self-sabotage.

At the beginning of each week, look at the blocks of time you've committed to working toward your goal and loosely schedule in the tasks and projects you need to accomplish. One thing I can say is that, if you think a project is going to take a week, it's probably going to take two. If you thought you could date fifteen different people in a month to find Mr. or Ms. Right, you probably need to relax that schedule. If you think you can build a huge social network in three weeks, you'll probably be disappointed. If you thought you could get something done in a day or a month, don't beat yourself up for the times that you can't. Stuff happens. Don't make organizing your time and laying out goals a way to beat yourself up. Sometimes, you simply won't be able to accomplish things within the timeframe that you think you should. As Mary Kay Ash says, *"A good goal is like a strenuous exercise—it makes you stretch."*

> As Mary Kay Ash says, "A good goal is like a strenuous exercise—it makes you stretch."

After you have your quarterly and weekly priorities written down, next be clear about what you want to get done for each day. What works really well for me is to write down the next day's tasks at night before I go to bed. I also set the alarms in my phone the night before for any appointments that I have the next day. (I know this sounds crazy, but when I get busy, I get caught up in the moment. An important appointment can easily get lost in the shuffle.)

Doing this the night before has all kinds of advantages. First of all, it lets you sleep better. By writing it all down, your mind won't start racing trying to remember what you need to do the next day. It also lets your unconscious start working on your tasks for tomorrow, coming up with creative ideas and solutions for you while you sleep. Then when you get started the next day, you feel clear about what needs to get done and can jump right in. You're much less likely to get caught up in all the things that rush in at you.

I don't create a To Do list but a Hit List of the top three things that I'd love to get done, then the one thing that, no matter what, I *have* to get done that day so I can feel accomplished. You can write down two or three, but what's the one major thing that is the most important? By writing it all down, if you cross off at least that one "must-do" thing each day and check off those boxes of other important tasks you completed or worked on, you start to be aware of the progress you're making. You'll feel like you're accomplishing something, not just spinning your wheels. It keeps you on track so that you don't get caught up in busyness but stay focused on actions that will make an impact. (By the way, if your Hit List has 15 items on it, you're trying to do way too much or you're not fully focused on what you really should be doing! And you'll never be able to finish them so you'll be self-sabotaging yourself because your brain will say, "See? You didn't finish your hit list again. This stuff must not be that important.")

Next, I time block each task or project. I look at the amount of time I've devoted to my different goals and schedule my Hit List into it. For example, I may use the hours of 9AM to 11AM for working on my next book. I schedule the specific things I want to accomplish for the book into that day. If I'm dedicating 2 hours a day to updating my training materials, I might schedule the specific scripts I need to write or videos I need to do between 12PM and 2PM the next day.

I've learned a couple of helpful tips for this. First, I always tell my students to do the most difficult thing first. Brian Tracy talks about this in *Eat That Frog*. He says to think of each task as a frog and that you should eat the biggest and ugliest frog the first thing in the morning. Why? When you do the most difficult thing first, it keeps you from procrastinating and making up excuses for not getting it done. Also, it feels great to get that ugly frog over with! It gives you your first big win for the day, that you tackled the ugly frog! Celebrate! Remember what gets celebrated gets replicated. It will make you feel energized and ready to tackle all the lesser issues. You also start to get more done because you realize that first ugly frog wasn't so bad after all. You recognize your success and success breeds success.

Also, whenever possible, I make sure that I'm doing the things that require the most focus and brain power during my peak hours, those hours when I feel the sharpest. I happen to be a morning person, but some people are at their peak later in the day. We all have individual daily rhythms where our energy is naturally high and then other times where we're naturally more relaxed. Figure out what your natural rhythm is and if possible, match your most difficult tasks to the time of day where your energy is highest.

Pomodoro Technique

By the time I get up in the morning, I've got the day all scheduled and I'm ready to go. Then there's one more layer I use to make sure I'm super-productive for the day. It's called the Pomodoro Technique. If you're struggling with time right now, if you don't feel like you have enough of it, if you are feeling like there's just never enough hours in the day, if you're working yourself like a crazy person, try this out. It really works, and I now teach it to all my students.

This technique was developed in the 1980's by an entrepreneur named Francesco Cirillo and, according to studies, you can get 16 hours more work done in a week by doing it! When I do the Pomodoro Technique, I start by setting myself up in a distraction-free zone. I turn off all notifications from my cell phone, Facebook, texts, *everything*. I totally screen all phone calls.

The technique itself is pretty simple. You look at the task you've got scheduled then set a timer for 25 minutes. During that 25 minutes, if something not related to what you're focused on pops into your mind, you write it down, but don't do anything about it. Keep your focus on the one task in front of you and when the time is up, get up and stretch and walk around for 3 to 5 minutes. Then set the timer for another 25 minutes and focus again. When the time is up, take another 3 to 5 minute break. Four of these segments (25 minutes of focus and 3-5 minutes break) is called one pomodoro. After one full pomodoro, you take a 15 minute break and answer emails or respond to texts or fold the laundry or just take a breather. If doing 4 pomodoro sessions in a row is too much, just start with one 25 minute stretch of total concentration and add more as you can. You'll be amazed at how much more productive and efficient you are with just being super hyper-focused for 25 minutes.

Even though we've all got phones with timers on them, Francesco Cirillo suggests using a mechanical timer. The timer he originally used was a kitchen timer that was shaped like a tomato. (Pomodoro is tomato in Italian!) He says the physical act of winding the timer is a physical signal to your nervous system that you're determined and ready to start that specific task. The ticking keeps you on track and the ringing is like a celebration that you accomplished something and it's time for a break! I've also found that it's best not to use a timer that you can *see* ticking because then you'll look at the time to see how much you have left (and that is distracting you and taking you off your task). I recommend that you buy a timer that you set, and it just goes off when the time is up but you can't see how much time is left on the clock. That way you're not tempted to take yourself away from what you are doing and look at the time.

For example, I might set up "Checking and Responding to Emails" as a 25-minute task. Or I might set up "Researching X, Y, Z" as my task. Maybe it's working on a PowerPoint presentation or brainstorming ideas for content for your videos. The task can be something that takes just one 25-minute period or a project that takes several. The point is to do just that one thing for the entire 25 minutes without allowing any distractions. You'll be amazed at how productive you feel and how much you accomplish!

If you don't use the Pomodoro Technique, you still need to pay attention to the segments of your time and use them wisely rather than just floating through the day. You can still say, "Hey, I have one hour right now. I'm going to spend the next 60 minutes working on this specific activity. I'm not going to answer my phone. I'm not going to check my text messages. I'm turning all my notifications off, and not checking Facebook." Unplugging from all that helps so much! During that hour as you think of other things that you need to do, just write them down but don't try to do them. Just stay focused on the specific task you started. If you stay laser-focused for a single hour, you'll produce so much more than several hours where distractions pull you every which way.

Track Your Results and Own Them

One thing I hammer into my coaching clients is that you have to track your results! To make sure the action you're taking is effective, you always want to be asking, "Is this action taking me where I want to go?"

What kind of response is your marketing campaign getting? Are you getting healthier and more fit on your new exercise and eating plan? How are your kids responding to the way you're communicating with them? Is the way you're managing your money helping you reach your financial goals? Are those courses teaching you what you need to know to progress in your career? Does the time you're spending with your significant other feel satisfying to the two of you?

Once you see the results you're getting, you need to own them! By that I mean you can't sit around blaming the economy, your competition, the weather or the alignment of the stars for any poor results you're getting. You need to take responsibility for those results and make the necessary changes to your actions to improve those results. Remember that famous quote? "Insanity is doing the same thing over and over and expecting different results." Einstein may or may not have been the one to say it, but it's still genius!

When I started my coaching and training business a few years ago, I noticed that I was frequently losing employees. I'd spend a lot of time training them only to have them leave and start their own businesses. Rather than blaming them, I took a look at myself and realized that I needed to improve my leadership skills. I took classes and got some good coaching in that area. Today, I've got terrific team members who love their jobs and our company. If I hadn't owned my responsibility for the previous turnover, my staff and my training company wouldn't be where it is today.

My husband and I recently went through a rough patch. We love each other like crazy but we just weren't connecting, and I was feeling lonely. I realized that, rather than just trying to be okay with it (and feeling miserable), I had to change how I was dealing with it. I had to step up and say something. I had to find the courage to tell him how I felt. Once I did, everything turned around and we're happier than we've ever been. But I had to own up to what I was doing, the way I was playing it, was *not* getting the results—a fulfilling and loving connection with him—that I really wanted.

By tracking the results you're getting, you can make course corrections and change your approach. Stay in love with your purpose and your why but be flexible about how.

Taking Care of Yourself

It may seem weird to talk about personal self-care when the topic is how to take effective action. But it's impossible to take effective action toward your goals if you're running on empty! I used to think personal self-care meant being self-indulgent. To me, it was like wealthy heiresses spending half the day getting massages and pedicures then spending the rest of the day sunbathing at the pool. I'm the kind of person who has always been a hard worker and I tend to put others first. So, spending time on "personal self-care" seemed really selfish.

But I came to realize it just means keeping all parts of yourself—physical, mental, emotional and spiritual—healthy and happy. Taking care of yourself is not selfish. It's necessary. It's like when the stewardess tells you to put on your oxygen mask first before trying to help someone else. That's not selfish, it's just smart. In that situation if you try to help someone else *before* taking care of yourself, not only will you probably die but you won't even be able to help, right?

When pursuing important goals, you will have to sacrifice some things like bingeing on Netflix every night or playing three rounds of golf every week or window shopping at the mall every weekend. But if you sacrifice your personal well-being, you may reach your goal, but you'll be miserable. How often have you seen high-powered executives sacrifice their health and their marriages in pursuit of building an empire? That's not the kind of success you want. Plus, when your body or your mental/emotional state is not healthy, you just aren't operating on all cylinders. The decisions you make won't be the best. Your communication with others gets strained. You simply can't be as productive.

Now, I'm still not into daily massages (though more power to you if you are!) but I still make sure that I "fill my tank" by taking care of the basics and coach my students to do the same by:

Getting some exercise: No matter what your physical shape, you need some kind of exercise in your routine to stay healthy and alert. We talked about this earlier in this book as well because it is so important! Exercise is a really effective way to deal with anxiety or uncertainty or depression. Studies have shown that people who exercise regularly feel more energetic throughout the day and feel more relaxed and positive about themselves and their lives. They also sleep better at night and have sharper memories. And you don't need to be a fitness fanatic to get the benefits! Research shows that even modest amounts of exercise can make a big difference.

Eating well. Okay, I know how it is. When times get stressful, a big bowl of Chunky Monkey sounds awfully good. We all want a little comfort food and that's fine. But a diet of Doritos, chocolate cake, and Pop Tarts won't really give you the fuel you need to keep your brain sharp, your body energetic, and your attitude upbeat. When we're stressed, we crave sugars and saturated fats. But after the initial high, those foods make us crash. Our stress, grouchiness, and anxiety actually increase.

I'm not saying you shouldn't have treats. But healthier food will make you feel physically, mentally and emotionally better and more capable of dealing with the challenges we're all facing right now. If you don't believe me, try a couple of days of full-on junk food, and see how you feel. Then try some days of healthier eating and notice the difference.

Connecting with others: Loving and feeling loved are so important to our well-being! Connecting with our friends, family and loved ones on a regular basis not only feels good, it also affects our brains. When you stay disconnected from the people you care about for any period of time, research shows that it impairs your executive function that controls thoughts and impulses. You become more impulsive, more anxious, and less resilient emotionally.

Getting enough good sleep. Your body and your brain need good sleep! I'm sure you know this from your own experience. For most of us, if we don't get enough sleep, especially if it's for several days in a row, we feel cranky, foggy-headed, and sluggish. Pay attention to what your body is telling you. Schedule yourself to get the hours of sleep at night that's right for you. For most people, that's 7 to 8 hours but your optimal amount may be more or less.

What if you wake up at night and can't get back to sleep? That's pretty common. Our brains get over-stimulated with all of our technical gadgets and the information blasting at us. Some of us wake up thinking of solutions to all of our daily challenges. Others have their brains spinning with anxiety and worry. You can find a zillion ideas online to help with this but a friend of mine came up with one that's really great for mindset:

Rather than counting sheep, he uses the alphabet. For each letter of the alphabet, he comes up with at least 5 positive words that he could use to describe himself. For example, A might be awesome, alert, alive, aware, audacious. B might be bright, blissful, brainy, beautiful, bold. Get the idea? He says that he usually falls asleep by M or Q. And when he wakes up in the morning, he's in a great mood! (Before you try this, you may want to look up some X words!) (I have to admit, I'm not the best person to give advice on sleep. Right now, I'm going through menopause and sleeping is rough, but I'm working on it. BTW, why do women have to have all the yucky stuff? Periods, menopause, easier weight gain, UGH!!)

Making time for fun: There is plenty of research that shows that having fun and leisure time can make us more productive and less stressed. On the flip side, studies have shown that people who don't have fun at least every once in a while end up more stressed and depressed. I know how it can be when you're cranking on an important goal. Taking time off to goof off seems like a total waste of time! But if you keep your nose to the grindstone *all* the time, you're bound to hit burnout at some point. And how much effective action can you take then?

Having fun, especially active fun like playing a game or going boating rather than watching a movie, has a ton of benefits. Having fun increases your creativity and stimulates imagination. It triggers endorphins which not only make you feel good but can even help with physical pain! Fun boosts your energy level so you feel more vital and alive. As George Bernard Shaw said, "We don't stop playing because we grow old; we grow old because we stop playing."

Taking care of yourself means that you're taking care of the only person who can reach your goals in life: *you*. *You* are your most important asset. *You* are the only one who can create the life you deserve to have. *You* are the only one who can take effective action toward what you want. If you really want to succeed, you need to treat *you* with the same care you would treat your most precious child or beloved significant other.

Becoming the Best Person You Can Be

"What you get by achieving your goals is not as important as what you become by achieving your goals."— Henry David Thoreau

It's easy to look at people who have had "overnight success" and feel envious. I always laugh when I hear someone describe me as an "overnight success". When I tell them I'm not, they'll say, "But you built a multi-million-dollar coaching business in under a year!" That's true but it doesn't tell the whole story. I had to *become* the person who could successfully build that business first—and that took a *lot* longer.

Here's the reality: First, most "overnight success" that you see took years and years to put together! Second, people who achieve success too quickly in *any* area can't usually handle it. They fly high for a while then crash and burn. Be grateful if your career or business hasn't been an overnight success or that you didn't immediately meet the person of your dreams. It's giving you the time to grow into the person you need to be. Success is not meant to be instant.

What people don't understand is that your outward success can't come faster than your own personal and professional growth. If it does, in many cases, it won't be sustainable because you won't be the kind of person who can deal with that success. In fact, instant success is often more a curse than a gift. Think of all those lottery winners who win millions of dollars by simply buying a ticket one day. Statistics say that *70% of them end up broke within 7 years*! Why? Because they hadn't grown enough as an individual to be the kind of person who could handle such a big windfall.

We have definitely become a microwave culture. We expect our on-line orders to show up within days or hours. We get news within minutes of an event happening. We can Google anything and get instant answers to our questions (though oftentimes the answers we get aren't really what we need or want or are just plain wrong!). And now some people even expect the success they desire to come in the time it takes to reheat a bagel! And when it doesn't, they get cranky and wonder what's wrong.

For my "overnight" success, I spent years to become the kind of person who could run the businesses I now have. I needed to build up my confidence. I needed to build up more knowledge so that I had more to share and could be a great coach. I had to rub elbows with high-powered coaches until I felt worthy of doing what they were doing. I had to work on public speaking and training skills. I had to learn leadership skills to successfully mentor the team I needed for my business. I had to overcome my fears as I entered the business and started investing heavily in it.

If I hadn't done all of that work, I might have stumbled into a few successes. But there's no way my business would keep growing and be sustainable today. And I know I'd be stressed and totally out of balance in my life.

Instead, because I did that work, I can honestly say that I love my life. I work hard and have grown along with my businesses. I appreciate facing a challenge because it means that I am still growing. I never want to stop feeling the good kind of overwhelmed because that means that I am stagnant and not growing. I've worked on myself personally so I can honestly say I'm a better mother, wife, friend and coach as well as a better leader in my businesses.

Instead, because I did that work, I can honestly say that I love my life. I work hard and have grown along with my businesses. I appreciate facing a challenge because it means that I am still growing. I never want to stop feeling the good kind of overwhelmed because that means that I am stagnant and not growing. I've worked on myself personally so I can honestly say I'm a better mother, wife, friend and coach as well as a better leader in my businesses.

That's why in my trainings, I emphasize personal growth as much as the nuts and bolts of building their businesses because I know one cannot outpace the other. A person who achieves a big level of success without growing as a person is often miserable and their success is short-lived. The only way you can make long-lasting changes and achieve true success is by growing into the person that success requires.

You can't get healthy and fit until you become the person who believes they can do it, makes a commitment and does what it takes—like eating healthy foods, exercising, and getting good rest. You can't be truly successful in business until you believe in yourself and master the professional and interpersonal skills you need. You can't have a great relationship until you decide you really want one and become the kind of person who can be a great partner. So, along with teaching how to do things like digital marketing, sales funnels, and client retention, I also coach students on mindset, life balance, and finding their purpose. In fact, many of them credit the personal growth work we do for a lot of the business success they're experiencing.

I believe that we always need to be growing as individuals. If you aren't, the life you're creating for yourself will either stay stagnant or fall apart. If you look around at nature, all living things are either growing or they're dying, one or the other. Nothing stays absolutely still for any length of time. And if it *does* stay still for too long, like a pond that stops flowing in and out, it gets stagnant, even toxic and starts dying. This is true in relationships, in businesses, in health and fitness, spirituality—any area you can think of.

If you want to create an amazing life, you can't think of yourself as a loaf of bread that only rises to a certain point then it's baked and done! You're never done! You need to keep becoming better and better versions of yourself. That means that along with setting goals for your career, relationships, health, etc., you want to make sure to set goals and take action in your personal growth. Following the suggestions and doing the exercises in this book and making them part of your daily routine is a great start. Treat it as the beginning of your journey and continue to find ways to grow.

An Attitude of Service

One of the ways we can really grow as people and find true success in life is to have an attitude of service. For me, helping people is what it is all about. I'm a person that just loves people. I love helping people and making people smile. That's why I was a third grade schoolteacher and why I got into real estate. It's why I do the coaching I do and write the books I write now. Helping people is in my nature. In fact, if you read my personal manifesto, half of it isn't even about me, it's about the people that I serve.

As Zig Ziglar used to say, "You can have everything in life you want, if you will just help other people get what they want." All of the highly successful people I've met who are happy and fulfilled in life would agree, and it's been key to my own happiness and success. My motto has always been, "People before things. Take care of people and the things just come."

About 15 years ago, Bob Burg and John D. Mann wrote a book called *The Go-Giver* that talks about this. People often think they need to be "go-getters" to be successful. They think they have to be cut-throat, focus on beating out the competition and getting as much as they can for what they offer. They're focused on what they *can* get out of their career or a relationship or friendship, not what they can give.

But research shows that people who concentrate on giving and serving are actually more successful in life than those who don't! Adam Grant, a professor of organizational psychology at Wharton, wrote a book called *Give and Take* that talks about dozens of studies on the power of generosity. He said, "I had many data points showing that the most successful people in a wide range of jobs are those who focus on contributing to others. The givers often outperform the matchers—those who seek an equal balance of giving and getting—as well as the takers, who aim to get more than they give."

I teach this principle to all my students—to contribute, to serve not sell, to offer as much value as possible—and, after they understand it and apply it, they're blown away by the results. Being a giver and having an attitude of service doesn't mean you need to sacrifice your goals or your own happiness. It doesn't mean you let people take advantage of you. Being a giver is the conscious decision to *give more value* than you expect to get back.

You have to take your eyes off yourself and put it on others. Have you ever been on a date where you spent the whole time worrying about how you were coming across? Or given a presentation where you were sweating bullets hoping that the audience liked you? When you focus on yourself, not only does it add a ton of pressure, but it makes you less effective. It keeps you from showing up as your authentic self and prevents you from connecting to others.

I used to be petrified whenever I had to speak in public. Before, it was all about, "Am I doing this right? Do they like me? Do I look okay?" Now, my main concern is what my audience needs, what benefit I can give them, and connecting with them.

Take your eyes off yourself. Serve others. Your generosity will be returned to you tenfold!

Launch Story

During the time I was writing this book, I was invited to join the Mastermind Launch challenge that Tony Robbins and Dean Graziosi were putting on. It was literally the largest affiliate launch in the world.

An affiliate launch is when someone asks others (affiliates) to promote their product or service. You team up with them to promote their product either because you just want to do them a favor or you really believe in their product or because you get paid some kind of commission. I had never done one before—and I was starting with the largest affiliate launch *ever*!

When they asked me, I knew that doing this would be really, really good for my brand in personal development and business coaching and consulting. Tony Robbins has been in the personal development space for around 45 years, and I think Dean's done it for 20 or more. In this launch challenge, the top ten affiliates would get to go to a five day mastermind with Tony and Dean and the other top affiliates. That alone, that experience of being around those kinds of marketing brains and people that have achieved such greatness, was incredible.

Wouldn't you pay a million bucks just to be a fly in the room with Tony and Dean?

I was excited and talking about this opportunity to one of my best friends and she mentioned that she knew someone who had worked for them, and this person had said that they didn't treat her well so she had left the company. Remember when I had said that I would never do anything that goes against my principles? That really shook me up. As much as I wanted to do this, and as much as I respected Dean and Tony's teaching, I couldn't be part of it if behind the curtain, they didn't treat their people well. It hurt my heart to think these people that I've had on a pedestal for so long maybe weren't what they claimed to be.

I was totally bummed but I had to stay true to myself, so I called the woman in the organization who had invited me to join the launch. "Hey, I don't think I'm going to be a good fit" and I explained why. She said, "Listen, I respect what you're saying and you're right. You're not a good fit if you feel that way. But can I just be honest with you? That's *not* the experience I've had at all. I'm on a personal cell phone basis with them and they're absolutely amazing. They treat all of us with respect. They're amazing family men and really walk their talk. So, in my experience, what you heard is really not the case." I was so relieved to hear that! And I told her I'd get back to her.

The next thing I needed to be sure about is whether the program they wanted me to promote would actually be good for my students. I wasn't going to do this just because it would be so great for me and my career. It had to benefit my students as well. Being of service to others is another of my strong values. So, I went through the first half of the program and OMG! It was awesome! It was so aligned with what I teach. They had brought in trainers and teachers for this program that I had literally spent hundreds of thousands of dollars to get coaching from. Russell Brunson was teaching in the course, and I've paid him over $250,000. Alex Hormozi was in the course, and I'd paid him $25,000 for just eight hours of coaching me. I mean, the people in the program are amazing trainers and coaches —not to mention Tony and Dean. So, I thought, "This is awesome!" I called and said, "Yes. Absolutely, I'm in!"

And what happens next? The Bad Wolf comes to town. See, I was competing against people that had millions of followers, people like Ed Mylett, Brendon Burchard, Tom Bilyeu, and my own mentor, Russell Brunson. As the Bad Wolf was happy to point out, I'd literally be competing with people that would be almost impossible to beat! They all have millions of followers and people on their email lists. I have a list of about 30,000 active people who open up my emails. In fact, many of the people who I was competing against were so well-known that they were actually featured in the training program we were promoting!

My Bad Wolf kept saying, "What makes you think...What are you doing?... You aren't in their league... There's no way that you're going to be able to beat Russell Brunson." For God's sake, he is my mentor. I know he has millions of followers. He has huge influence. He has a personal friendship with Tony Robbins and Dean Graziosi. That's how high up the chain these people are that I'm competing against. And so, I had to really completely change my mindset. I had to remember my *why*. I had to just visualize what I wanted and stop thinking about all the obstacles.

I gave myself a good talking to: "It *is* possible. You have a really strong influence, and you love your people, and you would never do anything you don't believe in. This program will really help and support them. By winning this launch challenge, you'll get to be in the room with some amazing people. So just keep believing that this can happen. Just do it."

I started visualizing myself at a long rectangular table with Tony and Dean. Tony is at the head of the table and his wife is to the right of him. I'm next to her and my husband, Steve, is next to me. Dean and his wife are across from us, and Russell Brunson and his wife are next to them. It's weird because my visualizations have never been as vivid as this one was! I could feel it and taste it. I literally was *at* the mastermind. I just kept seeing it and I kept believing. I quit saying I couldn't do it and started saying "I'm doing it!"

Even so, I have to confess to you that almost every single day, I'd panic even if it was just for a moment or two. This was bigger than just about anything I had ever done! I was getting emotional whiplash from feeling positive and excited one minute and to needing to Stop,

Snap and Switch from some crazy negative thought. Even after years of working on this stuff and strengthening my mindset, a bigger challenge always calls up bigger fears. But I knew that fear was just the Bad Wolf rearing its ugly head again. So I kept believing and visualizing and taking action.

I made a big mistake at first (one of several that I'm going to share with you). At first, I was just trying to get into the top 10, and quite honestly it seemed like a huge stretch even to get in the top 10. There are two phases to the launch challenge. The first phase is to see how many people you can encourage to sign up for the free 5-days of teaching. The second phase is to see how many of your people actually buy into the program. I should have been focusing on being in the top ten of that *first* phase first. By the time that first phase ended, I was number 14 based on the number of people I had brought to the free session.

I looked at that and my first thought (from the Bad Wolf, of course!) was, "So, there's no way I can get to the top 10 in the second phase from here! Just look at the math. *How* am I ever going to do it?"

And suddenly, I realized I was asking the wrong question. "How" will always mess you up. You need to be asking "why" not "how." With a strong enough why, you'll always figure out a how. I had to stop asking how, because when I asked how, it seemed almost too impossible. I had to just make the commitment to do it and just do the thing. So, I told the Bad Wolf to take a hike, and I kept visualizing *what* I wanted and *why* I wanted it. And as I did, I came up with more ideas for how to do it. And when the second phase of people buying the program started, the one that really counted, I was at number ONE on the leaderboard! I was so excited!

But that's when I made another mistake. I kept visualizing myself as number *two*, because doing the math and looking at it logically, I didn't think there was any way in the world I'd be able to beat Russell Brunson and a few of the other heavy hitters who had millions of followers and a huge email list. I was number one for a little over two days and then all of a sudden, Russell Brunson went up to number one and stayed there for a couple of days!

I caught myself and thought, "Krista, he's number one because you've been visualizing yourself as number two. You've got to visualize yourself as number one!" I did and literally, Russell and I went back and forth for about a day and a half. Russell was in the lead, then I was in the lead, then Russell was in the lead. Then after a day or so, I remained in first place until the last 8-10 hours! I was beating Russell! Then what happens? The next thing you know, this guy named Corby shoots to the top and ends up staying at number one and winning the challenge! (I found out later that he had to join forces with another guy in the top ten during phase one because they figured it was the only way they could beat me!)

Was I disappointed? Well, maybe a little. I'm human after all! But the fact that I took second place is almost unbelievable. It doesn't make sense that I would be able to compete with people with millions and millions of followers on social channels. They have huge email lists. They're all influencers. For example, Ed Mylett has one of the largest podcasts in the world on marketing. And I realized that the reason I beat almost all of them is because I've offered so much value to my students over the years. I've helped and supported them. They trust me so I was able to influence and persuade them in an ethical way to do something that I absolutely believed would help them. My list was much, much smaller, but my leads were actually stronger because of the trust they have in me. And *that* makes me feel awesome!

When I found out I was number two, I celebrated how far I'd come, from "This is impossible" to "I did it!" I had used every trick in my mindset playbook—staying to my values, ignoring the how and finding my why, affirming and visualizing what I wanted, stopping the Bad Wolf in his tracks, making mistakes and correcting them, an attitude of service—and that had taken me farther than I thought I could ever go.

When you have a dream or goal, you've got to believe in it, and you've got to see it and you've got to visualize it and you've got to keep visualizing it. I have to tell you, the mental struggle that I had in my brain during that two week timeframe was crazy! "Why are you doing this? You shouldn't be doing this. What makes you think you can win? There's no way you're going to be able to win." I had to constantly Stop, Snap and Switch. I had to Stop, Snap and Do rather than worry. I had to Stop, Snap and Believe that I could do it. I had to Stop, Snap and Remember times I'd overcome the odds before. I had to Stop, Snap and Visualize what I wanted.

I hope this story shows you that using these mindset practices and principles is *not* something that, once you learn them, life's going to be easy all the time and you're not going to have to practice them. It doesn't mean that you're not going to still have negative thinking because you are. Like me (who teaches this stuff!), you're still going to have negative thinking. It doesn't mean that you're bad. It just means that you need to be aware of it so you can work on it more. It's going to be a practice that you literally incorporate into your life all the time. And the more that you incorporate it, the easier it becomes to do it. But it's still a lifelong practice.

Final Words

"You will never win if you never begin."
—Helen Rowland

I t's so easy to flip open a book and think, "Yeah. Those were some great ideas." Then you get all wrapped up in your day and forget completely about it. It's not that you're lazy. We're all juggling a lot in life. But just hearing about these great ideas is not going to help you keep or get a healthy mindset. You have to actually *implement* the techniques and exercises. Remember, knowledge isn't power, implementation and execution is.

It's not like you can read one book or do one exercise or go to one workshop and your mindset will be strong and healthy and you live happily ever after. No! For most of us, it's something you need to work on all the time. I've spent years working with my mindset and years teaching it. I've become the Queen of Mindset—and yet I still need to keep at it. Read this book over and over. I'm the one writing it, and each time I go through it, I learn something new!

For example, one morning recently I woke up and I don't know what it was, but I was just in a funky mood. I felt really negative. I was thinking negative things like, "Why didn't Steve (my husband) do what I asked him?" and "We should be farther along right now in the marketing project we have going on." It was like a spiral of negativity swirling around in my thoughts. All of the sudden, I caught myself and I thought, "What's going on? What are you doing? Why are you being negative right now?" I recognized the spiral I was on was about to bring me down further, so I started playing the affirmations I've created to change my brain activity. It's a recording that's in my own voice saying positive things. And the rest of the day I was as mindful as

I could be about what I was saying to myself. I grabbed my Stop, Snap and Switch bracelet and was extra vigilant about what I was thinking the rest of the day.

Feeling negative is normal. We can't always be perfect and happy all the time. But we don't have to just accept it and let it ruin our whole day. It's okay to have negative moments, but we don't want to let those moments turn into hours, or days, or weeks or months—or lifetimes. Just recognize where you are, and when things start to go into a negative direction, navigate yourself into a positive one using some of the techniques in this book. You have the choice to nip it in the bud by being willing to shift into a better mindset and do something different. You can shift a day that starts out crappy into a day that feels good and positive. Anytime you have a negative thought, you need to stop and recognize that negative thought. We know that thoughts become things, so we need to make sure our thoughts are good.

You have to know this: No one is coming to save you. You have to save yourself. You are the only one responsible for creating the life that you deserve, and you have to believe that you deserve it.

I'll tell you right now that on your way to success, you will have to sacrifice something. It might be money, time, resources, or that precious ego of yours! You may have to give up a dead end job to find a great one or a dead end relationship to find one that's amazing. You may have to give up being the big fish in your tiny pond to move into that bigger pond you've always dreamt of. And I'll tell you right now, it won't always be easy. You have to permanently move out of your comfort zone and throw away the key! You'll have some hardship and disappointment along the way. You'll get a few bruises and feel uncomfortable. Understanding this ahead of time will help you keep going.

Because that's what you need to do. You need to access your self-control and your pig-headed persistence! As Chet Holmes would say, "You have to learn to push through how you *feel* and *act on the promise you made to yourself!*" And it's your powerful mindset that will help you do that.

> "You have to learn to push through how you feel and act on the promise you made to yourself!"

Be kind to yourself. Know that this is a constant work in

progress. When you're having a bad day and you feel like you have to snap your bracelet a bunch of times, don't get mad at yourself. Just be happy and recognize that you're now aware of your thoughts. This is not something that you're going to learn in a day. But the more you do it, the more you practice it and the more you tell your family about it and your friends about it, the more it's going to start to become a part of who you are.

Today, people will remember something tough from my past and say, "Wasn't that awful when that happened, Krista?" I have to stop and think because I hardly even remember the incident they're talking about! My brain has gotten to the point where I don't even remember the bad stuff. I'm not living under a rock. It's just that I've gotten really good at filtering out the stuff that's not serving me and filtering in the stuff that does.

Your job—and mine— is just to stay more cognizant of the game. Becoming more cognizant of your thoughts and your actions and whether they serve you or not is half of the battle. So just keep on going, keep on trying, keep on practicing and you're going to be great. And I can't wait to see and hear about your results. Be sure to share your wins on your social channels and use the #StopSnapAndSwitch so I can see them, and you can share them with others.

Also, be sure to join the Facebook group so you can share your wins with other Stop, Snap and Switchers. Just go to Facebook and type in Stop Snap and Switch with Krista Mashore. Or go to http://www. facebook.com/groups/stopsnapandswitch

"Don't wish it was easier, wish you were better. Don't wish for less problems, wish for more skills. Don't wish for less challenge, wish for more wisdom."
          —Jim Rohn

Wishing you the best life has for you—

Krista Mashore

Have you gotten value from this book? If so, help me help others get that same value by leaving a review on Amazon. It would mean so much to me and help me be able to help more people. Thank you!

Are you ready to really build the mindset that will help you achieve limitless abundance? If so, turn the page and join our Seven-Day Challenge! We have three of them focused on eliminating the negative thoughts and beliefs that hold you back, using different tools to keep your mindset strong and positive, and preparing your brain to support your vision.

Visit KristaMashore.com/SSSBook to get access to your Stop Snap & Switch resources

- Stop Snap & Switch Playbook
- Copies of graphics mentioned throughout the book
- Exclusive training videos
- 5 Day Limitless Life Challenge

SCAN ME

Your Seven Day Challenges

"The best project you'll ever work on is you."
—*Dean Graziosi*

Most people do not follow through! They want to change but then they don't do what it takes to make that change happen. I can tell you are NOT one of those people because you turned the page! Since you're reading this book, I know you're the kind of person who wants to train your brain to have a Master Mindset. So, I know you're going to do the challenges.

Each day during these challenges, you're going to concentrate on just one part of your mindset and practice it. The days build on each other to help you build a really solid mindset foundation. The idea is to continue doing what you focused on the day before while you focus on a new practice each day. Remember that repetition is what creates mastery.

To give you support, we've set up a Facebook group where you can share what you're learning from this challenge and cheer on others who are on the same journey! Just go to Facebook and type in the search bar, Stop, Snap and Switch with Krista Mashore, or go to http://www. facebook.com/groups/stopsnapandswitch. Also, you want to track your progress with this. So, for each day, your playbook has space for you to journal about what happened as you practiced the techniques.

I set these up as 7 day challenges because we can commit to anything for just 7 days, right? Oh, and it's a great idea to invite a friend or family member to do this with you. Study after study shows that when you have an accountability partner, you're much more likely to finish! So, let's get started!

1st Seven Day Challenge

Day #1: Stop, Snap, and Switch from the Negative

Today the focus is just on being aware of your thoughts and feelings. Start the day by putting on your Stop, Snap and Switch band or bracelet as soon as you get out of bed. Then, each time you notice yourself having a negative thought during the day, stop and acknowledge it, snap the band, and switch it to the other wrist as you replace that stinky thought with something more positive. For example, if you notice, "Ugh. I'm so tired this morning," stop, snap your band and switch it as you say out loud, "I have all the energy I need and today will be a great day!" Yes, this might seem silly at first and you might forget sometimes but give it your best shot. See how many times you can catch yourself and Stop, Snap, and Switch your way out of negative thinking! And don't forget to journal about today in your playbook so you can track your progress. Stop here and do the activity, and I'll see you tomorrow. I'm so excited for you!! And if you haven't already, be sure to encourage a family member or friend to do this with you ☺

Day #2: Stop, Snap, and Celebrate the Positive

Today, you'll keep being hyper-aware of your thoughts and feelings. But today, you'll also pay attention to the *good* thoughts and feelings and celebrate them. Remember that "Success breeds success" and "What gets celebrated, gets replicated." We definitely want to start replicating all the good in our lives, so today you're going to Stop, Snap, and Celebrate! Every time you feel good about something or have a positive thought about yourself or others, stop and acknowledge it: "Hey, I just had a loving thought about my spouse." Snap your wristband and, as you switch it, give yourself kudos: "Good for me that I'm being so loving!" You're doing great, I'll see you tomorrow!! Can't wait to read about your successes in the Facebook group!!

Day #3: Burn Your Limiting Beliefs

Today, you're going to tackle limiting, negative beliefs about yourself. You just need to find 10-15 minutes toward the beginning of your day to get this started. Go to your playbook and turn to the page called Burn Your Limiting Beliefs and you'll see a few columns for you to fill out. In the first, list all the limiting beliefs you have about yourself. Remember, a limiting belief might seem *absolutely true* because the Bad Wolf wants you to believe it! If it's ever gotten in the way of what you really want, write it down. A limiting belief also might not seem like a big deal to you. Write it down anyway. Write down *anything* that makes you feel bad or that has kept you from doing things in the past.

When you've got your list, in the next column write down what that belief has *cost* you. What did you not do or try because of it? What dream died because you believed it? This is a really good reminder of why you *must* get rid of that negative belief.

Then in the last column, write down a more positive belief to re-place the old rotten one. If you said, "I'm horrible with my finances," you probably don't want to start with "I'm the Warren Buffet of my neighborhood." Maybe something more like, "I'm learning to manage my money and getting better all the time!" To help you remember your new positive beliefs, write them down on sticky notes and post them all over the house. Also, go to the Facebook group, Stop, Snap and Switch with Krista Mashore and share your new beliefs with the group!! This will encourage others to do the same!

Then take the list you just made of limiting beliefs and what it cost you and burn it! (Do NOT set your house on fire!) And during the day, whenever one of those old limiting, negative beliefs pop up, Stop, Snap, and Switch to your new belief.

Congrats! I'm so proud of you. You wouldn't believe how many people can't even keep to their commitments for 3 days, but you did!! High Five to you!! Be proud of yourself!! Stop here, work on this and I'll see you tomorrow.

Day #4: Put It All Together

It doesn't do any good to do a practice just once and move on. You need to repeat it over and over so that it becomes automatic. So today, you're going to make sure that you're doing all three practices again: Stop, Snap and Switch (from any negative thoughts). Stop, Snap, and Celebrate (any wins or positive thoughts). Stop, Snap and Switch (from any negative or limiting beliefs you have about yourself). Repetition leads to mastery!

Isn't this fun?! Make it fun!! Celebrate your success. I'm so excited for you. Stop here and I'll see you tomorrow.

Day #5: Rewrite Your Personal Story

Go to the page in your Limitless Abundance Playbook titled Rewrite Your Personal Story. Think about some of the difficult times you've had in your life. What is the story that you tell to yourself or to others about it? Write that story down under the Old Story column. Next, think about a different way you could perceive what happened. Could it have meant something different than what you thought it meant? What gifts have you gotten because of it?

For example, my friend Raquel severely injured her neck in an ATV accident. She had always been very active, but the pain kept her from doing anything, even taking long car rides. She flew all over the country going to different yoga studios to try to get the pain under control. When she finally got better, she realized, "Hey! I can help others get pain relief too!" She created a new career for herself working one-on-one with people with chronic pain. That never would have happened if she hadn't had the accident. She decided that the accident didn't mean she would be in pain forever, but it was an opportunity to be of service to others.

Once you've written both the old and new story, you know what to do! Every time you catch yourself telling yourself or someone else that old story, Stop, Snap and Switch to the new one! Stop here and come back tomorrow!! I can't wait to hear about your progress in the Facebook group!!

Day #6: Rewrite Your Stories About Others

We not only have negative stories about ourselves. We also have them about the people in our lives. "My husband never listens" or "My mother is such a nag" or "My kids are so sloppy." We may think we've got LOTS of evidence to prove these stories! But what if we told a different story? What if we gave them the benefit of the doubt or focused on appreciating them? These stories might change to "My husband may not be the best listener but he's totally loving and loyal" or "My mother has always loved me and only wants the best for me" or "My kids aren't the tidiest kids around but they're playful and creative and will be great adults."

In your playbook, find the page titled Rewrite Stories About Others and fill in the columns. Then, whenever you notice that old story about someone in your life pops up, Stop, Snap and Switch to the new one!

Then pay attention to the difference in how you feel—and how they react. And be sure to journal about your day in your playbook. You got this!! I'll see you tomorrow!!

Day #7: Rewrite Your Global Stories

Go to the Rewrite Your Global Stories page in your playbook. Your global stories are the negative generalizations you make about people or life. For example, "Life is hard" or "You can't trust lawyers" or "Teenagers are so self-centered these days." In the column that says Old Story, write down all of the negative stories you're carrying around, even if you're totally convinced that they are absolutely true! If you're like most people, your list will be pretty long! (If it isn't, are you sure you aren't missing some?)

Next, rewrite these stories under the New Story column. You don't have to go all Pollyanna on this but come up with a story that is more positive, like "Life is an adventure" or "Many lawyers are sincere and trustworthy" and "Teenagers are just figuring out how to become great adults." Any time during the day that your old story pops up, Stop, Snap, and Switch to the new one.

Okay, how was this week? Did you learn something about yourself? Do you feel a little better about yourself and your life? Good! (Give yourself a Stop, Snap and Celebrate for that!) Go to the Facebook group and share your new insights and wins. Look back through your playbook and celebrate the progress you've made! How about the people around you, your family and friends. Do they notice a "different you" and do they feel better as well? If so, ask them to join you!! Invite your friends and family, I promise it will help solidify your experience and you can hold each other accountable.

Now how about committing to just 7 more days to build your mindset even stronger and more positive? You can do it!! Look how far you've come!! I can tell that since you've made it this far, you're the type of person who is committed to truly having the best life possible for not only yourself but for those people around you!!

2nd Seven Day Challenge

Part of this week will be about cleaning up your environment so that it supports your healthy mindset. We'll also get into using your body to fire up your brain.

But I don't want you to forget the gains you've already made. Review the exercises from last week. If you missed any negative beliefs or negative stories, write them down now along with the new story or belief. Pay attention to your thoughts and Stop, Snap and Switch or Stop, Snap and Celebrate all day long! Make these new practices into habits so you have them at your fingertips automatically when you need them.

Day #1: Eliminate Mental Junk Food

For some people, this can be really hard at first! We're so used to turning on the news in the morning or jumping onto Facebook when we have a minute. So today, I want you to eliminate just 3 types of mental junk food that you've used. Maybe it's getting distracted by those text alerts about celebrity gossip. Maybe it's watching The Weather Channel to catch up on the latest natural disaster. Maybe it's bingeing on Real Housewives of New Jersey! Whatever you are feeding your brain that makes you feel down or numb or unmotivated, consider it mental junk food!

Choose your 3 to eliminate and **for the whole week** do not engage in them. And every time you get the urge but stop yourself, give yourself a Stop, Snap and Celebrate! And if you slip up and get sucked into what you're trying to eliminate, don't beat yourself up! Mental junk food can be addictive! So, just Stop, Snap and Switch when you catch yourself and look for some better food for your brain! And if 3 is too many, that's okay, just choose one or two. But be sure to at least choose one! Stop here, and I'll see you tomorrow. Great job by the way!

Day #2: Bring in Healthy Mental Food

Tony Robbins' mentor, Jim Rohn, told Tony that he should read something positive for 30 minutes every single day. He said, "Miss a meal if you have to, but don't miss a day of reading." These days, we can "read" by using audio books or listening to positive podcasts as well as actually reading books. Today, find some healthy mental food that you can have on hand for yourself. Then **every single day this week, "read" for at least 15 minutes.** And after every 15 minute healthy mental food session, give yourself a Stop, Snap and Celebrate! And be sure to journal about what you learned in your playbook.

Day #3: Your Negative Nellies

Don't worry, I'm not going to tell you to ditch your friends and family! But now is the time to really think about them and the impact they have on your life. Go to your playbook and you'll find a sheet that has 4 concentric circles. In the smallest circle in the center, write the names of the people who are closest to you, the ones who influence you the most like your immediate family or best friend. In the next circle, write the names of people who are close but not quite as close. Maybe these are friends you see often, or people who are important to you at work, or extended family. In the next circle, you might have co-workers and friends you see less often. And in the outer circle, you would have people in your life that have much less impact on you, like neighbors.

Next, think about each of these people and how they make you feel. Would you say they have a positive, negative, or neutral impact on you? Take out some highlighters and color code the names. Do you have more positive or negative people in your first two inner circles? "Negative" doesn't mean they are bad people. It just means that they do not support who you are becoming. Consider spending less time with those who bring you down and more time with those who lift you up. Write some notes in your playbook to capture what you've discovered.

Great job! Celebrate the fact that you've come this far! I'm excited for you!

Day #4: Stop, Snap and Superhero!

Today, you're going to play with ways your physiology can improve your attitude and mood. Start the day by trying out a few Superhero or Superheroine poses. Still holding that pose, announce what you have planned for the day. For example, stand like Wonder Woman with head held high and hands on hips, and announce, "I am going to meet with a new client today." "I am going to balance my checkbook today." "I am going to be super productive." "I am going to have tons of energy today." How does that feel? Don't you feel happier and more energetic? I know I do when I do it!!

Now, as you go through the day, especially if you're facing some challenges, find a few moments to strike your Superhero pose again. Have fun with it! I'll see you tomorrow, keep up the good work!!

Day #5: Stop, Snap and March!

Like yesterday, today you'll use your body to strengthen your mindset. Before the day gets started, practice walking with a strong, confident stride like you are a Very Important Person who is going to a very significant event. Just notice what that feels like and how it shifts your attitude.

Next, as you go through the day, every time you stand up to walk somewhere, march like a VIP on a mission. Because you know what? That's the truth of who you are! (If you have to tone it down a bit in the office, that's okay but still stand a little straighter and walk a little more confidently than you usually do.) Remember, nothing happens unless you actually do the activity. Be sure to share your successes with the Facebook Group!!! Keep up the great work and I'll see you tomorrow!!

Day #6: Attitude of Gratitude

Today, start and end your day by thinking of just 3 things you're grateful for. They can be things in your past or things in your present. They can be as simple as appreciating your morning coffee or feeling grateful for your health. Write them down and take a moment to really experience that good feeling of gratitude. And be sure to journal about it in your playbook. Stop here and feel grateful for whatever you've chosen. Then be ready to come back tomorrow. Be sure to share your "ah ha's" in the Facebook group and share your wins with the world!! #StopSnapandSwitch on your socials.

Day #7: Repeat and Celebrate

Today, you'll keep doing what you've learned in the past 14 days. Here's where we are so far: You're doing the Stop, Snap and Switch for negative thoughts and as well as negative, limiting beliefs that you have about yourself and others. You're doing the Stop, Snap and Celebrate for any minor wins during the day. You've eliminated 3 types of mental junk food and you are feeding your brain good stuff for at least 15 minutes per day. You're also practicing using your body to shift how you're feeling and tapping into gratitude every morning and night. Woo hoo! You're on a roll!

For me, doing these things has become a habit. They're just part of my everyday life. But I know that when you're starting out, it's hard to remember and old patterns kick in. To help you out, I'd suggest putting sticky notes all over to help you as reminders. Put one on your steering wheel that says, "Stop, Snap and Switch." Put one on your door so that as you leave the house, you see "Stop, Snap, and Superhero!" Put one on your mirror that says, "I am grateful for…" Put one on your computer that says, "Stop, Snap and Celebrate!" Use these reminders until the practices become automatic to you.

Are you starting to feel a difference in your mindset? A little more upbeat and positive? We're not looking for perfection here, just incremental changes. Every small step you take, every time you practice a technique, it builds your foundation. Celebrate your progress!

And now to take it even further, how about committing to just seven more days?

Don't forget to join the Facebook group. Just go to Facebook and type in the search bar, Stop, Snap and Switch with Krista Mashore, or go to http://www.facebook.com/groups/stopsnapandswitch. Also, you want to track your progress with this. So, for each day, your playbook has space for you to journal about what happened as you practiced the techniques.

You've already done two Seven Day Challenges. I'll bet you can do at least one more, right? Let's get started!

3rd Seven Day Challenge

This week, we're going to focus on your vision for your life. Without a vision and goals, most of us just wander. We let "life" decide who and what we're going to be. But not you!

Day #1: Creating Your Vision

Quickly re-read the vision section in this book then go to your Limitless Abundance Playbook and find the page that says Create Your Vision. You'll find the categories to think about and pages for you to write on. Don't hold back! Be bold about what you really want out of life! If your life was a 10 on the scale of 1 to 10, what would it look like? Have fun with this and don't let your beliefs about "impossible" get in your way!

Whoot Whoot, you're crushing it!! Stop here and I'll see you tomorrow. Be sure to share your successes in the Facebook group, I love reading those!!

Day #2: 7 Levels to Discover Your Why

I learned about this practice from Dean Graziosi's book, *Millionaire Success Habits*.

Today, we're going to take pieces of your vision and uncover why you want them. For example, you might have said, "I want to earn $200,000 per year." Okay, so why do you want that income? Maybe your response is, "I want to easily pay my bills each month and have plenty of money to put toward savings." Okay, why do you want to pay your bills each month and why do you want to build up savings? Maybe your response is, "Because I watched my parents struggle and I never want to feel the stress and worry they always felt." Now, you're starting to get to the heart of the matter.

Keep asking 7 levels of why you want each part of your vision until you have an answer that feels real and emotional to you. Having a strong why is key to getting where you want to go.

You're doing great!! Keep up the momentum. I'm sure you're noticing huge shifts in your happiness and mindset. Be sure to share your progress in the Facebook group. I promise it will help other people, and since you've come this far, that means you're the type of person who loves not only helping yourself but also loves helping others.

Day #3: Carrot and the Stick

Today, go back to your 7 levels of why and see if you can find a carrot and a stick for each thing you want. In the example about money, maybe the carrot is "I want to be able to travel the world and see places I've never seen" and your stick is "I don't want to feel anxious about money like my parents did." Notice which one, the carrot or the stick, is stronger and more compelling for you. Burn these whys into your mind so that, when the going gets tough (and it always does!), you'll know why you must keep heading forward!

I'm so excited for you!! Keep on going, stop here and I'll see you tomorrow. Can't wait to see your successes in the Facebook group.

Day #4: Checking in with Your Values

In your playbook, you'll find a page titled Identify Your Values. Start listing all of the values that are important to you. If you get stuck, think about times you were proud of yourself. What quality in yourself caused you to be proud? Were you courageous or compassionate or creative? Think also about times you were upset with yourself or others. Did it have to do with being irresponsible or thoughtless or sloppy? When you're upset, it's usually because some value of yours has not been met.

Now, take your list of values and compare it to your vision. Is there anything in that vision of things you want that does not fit your values? If so, how could part of your vision be changed or modified so that it does match your values?

Stop here, and I'll see you tomorrow. Keep crushing it!! Feel proud of yourself that you've made it this far!! Great work!

Day #5: Create Your Manifesto

Your manifesto is a short (not more than one page) compelling statement about your vision. It doesn't have all the details, but it has the most important parts and why you want it. Don't worry about the writing. This is for you to help you lock into your brain that this vision is your *destiny*.

When you have your manifesto, print out a few copies. Every morning and every evening, pull out your manifest and read it out loud. Be sure to post a copy of your completed manifesto in the Facebook group, it will help others and give them inspiration. I can't wait to see what you've come up with!! Celebrate your success!!! You're doing so well and by being here this long, it shows me that you're someone who is committed to mastery!!

Day #6: Create Your Affirmations

An affirmation is another way to build certainty into your mind. It's just a brief, positive statement that announces your desires and goals. It's in the present tense, not the future. It's something you can memorize and say or write down frequently throughout your day. Think of it as the truth in advance. Some examples: "I am a loving wife and mother who is patient, kind and understanding." "I have happy, satisfied clients who pay me over $350,000 per year." "I am toned, flexible, and strong and a trim size 8." You can also make it goal-specific: "As of August 21st 20XX, my business does $1.5MM in sales and has 4 new employees." "As of March 2nd 20XX, I am the proud owner of a new 3,000 square foot home on a 5 acre lot." "As of June 13th 20XX, I have completed my first novel."

Take the affirmations you've created and write them down so that you see them frequently. Repeat them to yourself as you're driving around or walking the dog. Record them in your own voice and play them while you cook dinner or as you fall asleep. Stop here, I'll see you tomorrow!! Can't wait to see your affirmations in the Facebook group!!

Day #7: See Your Success

You are a total rock star, truly!! You are one of the small percentage of the population that actually finish what they start. Great work!! Visualization is so powerful for creating the certainty you need to achieve your vision and goals! If you haven't done it before (or if you've only visualized the bad stuff that could happen!), it may take a little practice. You want to imagine a scene that shows you that your vision has *already been accomplished*. For example, in the launch challenge, I visualized having dinner with Tony and Dean and the other winners. If your goal is to be debt-free, you could visualize sitting with your checkbook writing out checks to credit card companies or seeing a bill come in that shows a zero balance. If your goal is to climb Kilimanjaro, you could visualize yourself at the top of the mountain giving high-fives to all the other climbers.

Make sure to get your visualization as vivid as possible. What does the air feel like? What are you wearing? Who else is there and what are they saying? Let your brain really *see* it so it can believe it.

Ready for some other challenges? Be sure to remain in the Facebook group for more upcoming Challenges. And, if you felt this book and this Challenge was helpful. It would mean so much if you could refer a friend and talk about it on your socials. Also, by giving me a 5 Star Review on Amazon or Audible, it will help me help other people. I appreciate your time so much. Great job!! Whoot Whoot!!! I can't wait to hear how much using all the Stop, Snap and Switch techniques will change your life!! I love hearing the successes!!

I wish you the very best of luck on your Limitless Abundance Life!!!

Xxo

Krista Mashore